WRITING ACROSS CULTURES

A HANDBOOK ON WRITING POETRY AND LYRICAL PROSE

(FROM AFRICAN DRUM SONG TO BLUES, GHAZAL TO HAIKU, VILLANELLE TO THE ZOO)

EDNA KOVACS

BLUE HERON PUBLISHING, INC.
HILLSBORO, OREGON

WRITING ACROSS CULTURES:
A Handbook on Writing Poetry and Lyrical Prose

Published by

Blue Heron Publishing, Inc.
24450 NW Hansen Road
Hillsboro, Oregon 97124
503.621.3911

Melody Holmes, whose art graces the cover, was 12 at the time she produced the chalk pastel piece. She was enrolled in the Anna B. Crocker Program for Children & Young Adults at the Pacific College of Northwest Art.

Kovacs, Edna.
    Writing across cultures : a handbook on
writing poetry and lyrical prose : from
African drum song to blues, ghazal to haiku,
villanelle to the zoo / Edna Kovacs. —
Hillsboro, Or. : Blue Heron Pub., c1994

    p. : ill. ; cm.
    ISBN: 0-936085-25-8

    1. Poetics — Study and teaching.   2.
Creative writing — Study and teaching.   I.
Title

PN1101.K   808.1 dc20

ISBN: 0-936085-25-8

Library of Congress Catalog Card Number: 94-70211

CONTENTS

ACKNOWLEDGMENT

This book was made possible in part by an Education/Outreach grant from the Metropolitan and Oregon Arts Commissions with a matching grant from Blue Heron Publishing, Inc. The author wishes to thank the publishers, Dennis and Linny Stovall, and the interns, Erin Leonard, Frank Marquardt, and Dave Sorsoli, for being of the same nest.

Thanks to Barbara Drake, Gerry Foote, Dorothy McMahan, Doug Marx, Deborah Pearson, Kim Stafford, Joan Starker, and Rick Zenn for their letters of support and encouragement; to Judith A. Chambliss for her technical assistance; to the members of the Education/Outreach panel, members of the Commission, City and County officials, Alan Alexander III, Project Grant Program Manager, William D. Bulick, Director, and Donna Milrany, Associate Director of the Metropolitan Arts Commission for helping me realize my artistic vision; to Ellen Summerfield, Director of the International Studies Programs, Sandy R. Soohoo-Refaei, Assistant Director, Sandra E. Lee, Associate Professor of English as a Second Language, and the International Studies Department at Linfield College for their in-kind contribution and Cultural Awareness Week; to Dr. Fred Ross, Director of the Education Department at Linfield College for his interest and enthusiasm in this project.

Thanks also to Vincent Dunn, Peter Sears, and The Oregon Arts Commission; to Vicki Poppen, Lisa Barnes, Kathy Ems, and the Artists-in-Education program; to Lynn Lewis, Janice Ingersoll, and Young Audiences of Oregon, Inc.; to Sylvia Frankel, Director of the Oregon Holocaust Resource Center for her interest and assistance; to Nancy Nusz and the Oregon Folk Arts Program; to Jeff MacDonald, Director of the International Refugee Center of Oregon for his assistance with Iu-Mien Proverbs; to Sylvia Linington and the Metropolitan Learning Center Community Schools program.

My appreciation goes out to all the students, teachers, and staff wherever I have hung my teaching hat, particularly the English and International Studies Departments at Linfield College, the Northwest Writing Institute at Lewis and Clark College, the Oregon Arts Commission, and the Portland Public Schools, for giving me such a legacy of teaching experience to draw from, and to my own teachers, especially my fifth and sixth grade language arts teacher at Bret Harte Elementary School in Chicago, Illinois, Betty Bodian, who nurtured my innate writing talent, and my mentor, the late Canadian poet and playwright, George Ryga; and to Melody Holmes for her stunning cover art; artist Jana DeMartini Svoboda, Greg Ware, Director, and Donna Gamble, Assistant Director of the Pacific Northwest College of Art for their time and assistance in helping me choose the art which graces the cover.

Most of all, I am grateful to my parents, who have bestowed upon me a rich ethnic heritage, as well as instilling within me the commitment and desire to make teaching and learning a lifelong process — for in the words of my father: "You can lose all your friends, you can lose all your money; but you can never lose your education."

PREFACE

Because of a thickly-penciled child's composition I read long ago, I seldom walk on a beach without the impulse to shout Zoob. This is the way writing can work on the heart, tidelike and powerful, churning up sand and leaving its foamy impression.

Across a distance of 22 years, I recall my first teaching job at Washington Elementary School in inner-city Oakland, California. From the playground, you could look down the hill to the postcard panorama of San Francisco Bay, crisscrossed by the Golden Gate and Bay Bridges, dotted with boats, the City changing constantly from fog-draped to sun-puddled. Yet with all that visual feast laid out before those children, many of them had never been to the coast, barely out of eyesight and just an hour away. So my wife Jan, also a teacher at the school, organized a weekend field trip to the seashore for second graders. We gathered parents and friends, anyone with a car, and one Saturday morning caravaned to the beach, where the children played ceaselessly in the surf.

Back in the well-worn classrooms of school on Monday, children wrote about their adventure. Felecia's story is the one that has stuck in my memory since:

> "We went to the ocean and the suds chased us. Zoob, zoob, I feel good."

I'm not exactly sure why that little snippet of second grade writing has stayed with me all these years. Maybe I was struck with the expression of joy in the midst of a community that, mired in poverty, had more than its fair share of sorrows. Or maybe it was Felecia's invention of the word Zoob. Or maybe it was her use of "feel" rather than "felt," which expresses a recapturing on Monday of Saturday's joys, the chance to feel once more the warm breeze and the sand underfoot and the toe-numbing Pacific waves, to experience it all again as it is written, and then again and again as it is read and remembered. This deepening and extending of experience is one of the gifts writing can offer us.

Writing — a skill and tool as well as an art form — offers us plenty else besides. It is pragmatic and useful; it can help us get things done. It teaches us to be clear and to revise ourselves. It requires us to imagine the needs of others, our potential readers. It communicates across time and distance, offers permanence, and asks for the commitment to stand by our words. It is a cornerstone of civic engagement; our democratic tradition has writing — manifestoes, letters to the editor, voters' pamphlet arguments, speeches — at its heart. We can recognize all these practical and functional uses of writing, but we also can't deny its expressive and creative power, and that is the primary domain of this handbook. This is a book that makes this assertion: the experience of *zoobing* is far too rare in the world.

Writing Across Cultures offers plenty of poems, stories, and writing and teaching ideas. In these pages, Edna Kovacs has collected a huge range of forms and sources of writing, thus opening the door for the reader to glimpse the infinite breadth and variety of the craft.

The poems and stories aren't presented as objects for analysis so much as vivid works to be experienced and enjoyed and to serve as inspiration for our own or our students' subsequent explorations of writing.

In its scope and diversity, this collection celebrates a multiplicity of cultures, traditions, and poets. Any writer can use this rich source material to try on other voices, points of view, rhythms, attitudes, ideas and issues. This is significant practice at empathetic engagement with other lives, at imagining how others might feel, important capacities for all of us citizens of a multicultural world to enlarge. This book allows us to travel the world. From dense modernist poetry to sentimental cowboy ditties, from highly-structured verse to free-flowing wordplay, from historic and traditional forms such as the villanelle to present-tense and popular forms such as rap, and from every corner of the globe and many languages and peoples, poetry pours forth in this book.

In many sections, student writing samples are shared, a powerful demonstration that invites students, parents, teachers, and all apprentice writers into the discussion. These samples recognize young writers as part of our literary traditions. When young writers discover what their fellow students have achieved as writers, who knows what they will undertake?

In all these ways, and others, Edna Kovacs has made a handbook with vitality, music, range, depth, and diversity. In this book, poetry and lyrical prose are alive, rich, and culturally bountiful. Open the pages and enjoy, be inspired, try some writing yourself. Then share what you have discovered with your students or your friends. Then lean into your desk and write some more.

Zoob.

— Tim Gillespie, longtime teacher and writer and past president of Oregon Council of Teachers of English

INTRODUCTION

PLAYING IN A FIELD OF WORDS
An Invitation to Writing Across Cultures

You are now entering into a field of words. Please bring your children and your children's children, your perfect pet, a picnic basket, your fishing pole. In this field instructed with wild mustard, you may learn to live the day without a script. Here, you may dream every color that lifts you into freedom — be the silence unfolding with leaf-bud. Sometimes, whole mornings can get lost like this, setting out foot before daybreak. It is like a second sleep — rinsed in spruce pitch — with ducks that call in unison from beyond their peaceful pond. Out of the East, a red swan rises, at one with the sky.

Meanwhile, the outside world is rapidly becoming a global village, and cultural literacy is lacking. With school budget deficits and major funding cuts to prisons and mental health facilities, bigotry and racism on the rise, my response to this cancer growing in our society was to write a multicultural poetry and lyrical prose writing handbook to help open people's minds.

On May 3, 1993, I received an Education/Outreach grant from the Metropolitan and Oregon Arts Commissions to research, write, and edit *Writing Across Cultures* for people of all walks of life, ages 8–adult. Within the book are exercises and writing examples ranging from *African Drum Song to Blues, Ghazal to Haiku, Villanelle to the Zoo*.

To use this valuable resource, you must write from within. Classroom teachers should be advised that there are sensitive issues that poetry — and this book — deals with, such as AIDS, the Holocaust, and gender issues. Thus, it would be wise for teachers to be selective, reflective, and goal-based when choosing appropriate writing activities. For example, teachers who run high school writing centers have told me they would feel completely at ease having their students leaf through the book, choose an idea, and work independently at their computers. And elementary school teachers will find that individual and class books may be created from many of the suggestions offered here beginning with the warming up exercises and ending up at the zoo!

This book also aims to reach teacherless classrooms, outdoor school settings, community schools, remedial clinics, hospital classrooms, creative writing workshops, the deaf culture, exceptional children, home-schooled children, transitional learning projects, and multicultural studies programs.

Perhaps the reason why I wrote this book is because, growing up in the richness of Chicago's ethnic neighborhoods, I was fortunate to experience an awareness for cultural diversity. Being of Swiss-Hungarian descent, the youngest of five siblings, I grew up hearing the voices of Chinese, Hispanic, Greek, African-American, Eastern European, and Japanese immigrants. I have had good friends with names like Sim Der, Marcella Varella, and Norman Nakama. I took great delight in learning how to play Chinese jumprope and sing "Sakura." Years later, I would live and work in London, Cornwall, and Israel. Living on a kibbutz for eight months during the Arab-Israeli war, and subsequently living in Greece, heightened my interest in multiculturalism. Thus, as a teacher and writer, I am committed to passing this knowledge on.

Upon receiving my B.A. in Anthropology from Northwestern University, with an M.Ed. from the University of Illinois at Chicago with specific endorsement in learning disabilities, my teaching career was launched some twenty years ago.

With a teaching job in the offing with the Portland Public Schools, I followed my heart and moved west. I have had experience teaching crippled children, children with learning disabilities, educably retarded and emotionally handicapped children, blind children, children with lymphoma, acute myelogenous leukemia, cerebral palsy, dementia, Frederich's ataxia, Guillain-Barre syndrome, pregnant teenagers, ESL students awaiting appropriate placement, women on parole, latchkey, abused, and autistic children. During those years, while we worked on math, reading, social studies, spelling, and real-life skills, I always brought writing ideas. What amazed me, was that all of those students showed gifts when it came to expressing who they were — their deepest thoughts and wildest dreams — even if I had to write down the words.

Like a folklorist, I have collected student writings along the way. Students of all ages and all walks of life have entered into a field of words, exploring the vast world of their imaginations.

It was Whitman who wrote: "Slang is the voice of the people, and the strongest and sweetest songs yet remain to be sung."

I hear those voices all around me — and I am moved by them.

First, let's consider the children. Back in the early 1980s, when I neither owned a car or knew how to drive, I rode the bus to work. Being an itinerant teacher in the Portland Public Schools, I not only got to know the city well, you could say that I knew the bus map like the back of my hand, and I showed a great verve for guiding others to their purple raindrop, orange deer, brown beaver, yellow rose, or green snowflake destinations. I saw a lot of life from the windows of those Tri-Met buses. Each day was an epic journey.

My cases took me to every niche and cranny of this city — from a pool hall to a hospital classroom. I taught in libraries, church basements, under bridges, in burger bars. I kept a journal and wrote about what I saw:

CONSIDER THE CHILDREN

> She's a cocaine addict
> pregnant
> living with her son
> beneath the St. John's Bridge.
> Three days a week
> I buy him cheeseburgers, french
> fries, and chocolate milk at
> Burgerville — his only meal for the day.
> From his seat in the windowbooth
> he counts truck after truck.
> He loves trucks because
> his father was a trucker who died
> while driving too fast.

> > "Some day I'll be a trucker
> > just like him!"

> After lunch, we walk to the library
> where I teach him
> what he's spozed to know.
> His mind's on how to pimp
> for his mother. It's clear
> he feels responsible
> for their survival.
> I'm on to him when he darts
> into the Elk's Club and
> pickpockets a wallet
> from the coat rack.
> When I make him put it back
> he pulls down his pants
> in the middle of the street
> and screams obscenities.
> He's twelve years old,
> it's thirty-three degrees

in the middle of January.
He seemed happy the day he
grasped how to simplify fractions,
but on his way home he tossed
all his books into a trashcan.
He became a prostitute.

> "We gotta get by somehow!
> My momma's gonna have a baby!"

His momma's angry with the system
for kicking David out of school.
Though the characters and setting
may differ, the theme's the same:
the system's not working
for kids like David.
When I write up my reports
for the State, I think about
cave paintings no one will discover
until it's too late.

— *EDNA KOVACS, APRIL 1987*

And second, this piece about the homeless:

SILENCE AND TEARS

Some days I run away from home
to shiver with the homeless:

> "It's a beautiful day,
> and so are you!" the man
> by the river sings.

Before I go, I offer him
my blanket
afraid that out of pride
he won't take it.

But he does — and from the depths
of his frozen eyes
he thanks me for my
wide green meadow.

— *EDNA KOVACS, AUGUST 1990*

Several years ago, at a reading that was given by many outstanding Native American poets at Portland State University. I was particularly taken with the following remarks by Ed Edmo and Vince Wannassay.

Vince: I was looking at a sidewalk thinking you should be sand — I was looking at a telephone pole thinking you should be a tree — Money is God. God is money. This week I'm broke. This week I'm an atheist.
Ed: I came to the city and slept in phone booths when it rained.

While the real world has a lot of work to do we as poets and writers have the responsibility to sustain it. And while the world is full of the Blues we hear on radio, read about in newspapers and magazines, and encounter in our day-to-day lives, the Poet is always there to take notes in every language, in any season, and sings with a voice that must be heard.

And so I invite you to enter into this field of words — picnic on writing examples from writers of all ages and parts of the world. You may respond in poetry or prose form — in whatever language is yours. Many of these genres may spark a curiosity in you or your students to further explore the origins of many forms of literature. Your libraries, museums, and bookstores are rich troves of information and they await you. Wherever the brook flows, follow it. It is my hope that this book will encourage your appreciation for cultural diversity and better educate you for a brighter tomorrow.

For me, the writing of this book has been like cultivating a garden. Kahlil Gibran wrote: "Every seed is a longing." And while I share with you this joyful harvest, there is more work to be done. Gardening, like learning, is an ongoing process. I bring my hands to the garden and learn my place.

— *EDNA KOVACS, DECEMBER 3, 1993*

WARMING UP

WARMING UP

WARMING UP

WARMING UP

WARMING UP

WARMING UP

THOUGHTS ON POETRY & LYRICAL PROSE
A Word About the Writing Process

In the fall of 1992, I was asked to teach a literature class to Japanese exchange students from Kanto Gakuin University through the English and International Studies Departments at Linfield College in McMinnville, Oregon.

My poetry text was Kenneth Koch and Kate Farrell's *Sleeping on the Wing*. When students opened to the poems of Emily Dickinson, William Carlos Williams, W.B. Yeats, and others, they looked puzzled. Not only had they not studied poetry in Japan, they had never read poetry in English.

Several hands went up around the classroom. The question was the same: What is poetry and prose?

The following morning, I rose at dawn and drove to the Arboretum to gather autumn leaves, pine cones, bark, moss, lichen, twigs, and acorns that had fallen to the forest floor. When I arrived in class that day, with several sacks full, I told the students to close their eyes, reach into the bag, and select something from the grove. With their eyes closed, they were first instructed to smell. And when they opened their eyes, they explored the rest of their senses.

And while they reached into the realms of their senses, this is what I said:

> *There is no door to enter. Suddenly you find yourself on a deserted beach with the tide coming in. You could stand here forever with the moon or the sun. You could stand here remembering your childhood among the agates and driftwood with the far off scent of sea pine touching the wind. You could listen to the waters grow deeper and deeper — desire a path spun by fireflies to a kind of heaven. Close your eyes. Try to imagine.*

Smell, touch, see, hear, taste. Writing involves all the senses. I then instructed the students to write three short lines about the spruce cone, maple leaf, or feather they had recently discovered. By becoming absorbed in the process, they explored their inner voices, and wrote poem upon poem, story after story. For the rest of the semester, they were hooked on reading, writing, and discussing the literature of Shakespeare, Dickinson, W.C. Williams, and others — as well as their own.

Now it's my custom to ask students each fall to pick up a leaf — it will tell you what to say. Some students write their haiku on the leaves themselves, and enclose them as gifts in letters sent home to family and friends.

Being the sort of person I am, it's not unusual to find myself becoming just as absorbed as my students in doing my own assignments. Students appreciate teacher involvement.

The following are five leaf haiku written that autumn, while pondering how to answer that intriguing question — What is poetry and prose?

LEAF HAIKU

> I have no self today
> and the wind knows it —
> scraping me clean

> Here in this field
> of golden asters
> the dew knows me

> Upon waking
> the rain's heartbeat and mine
> are the same

> a sumac leaf am I
> dancing
> in September's fire

> Even fallen leaves
> hold the moon
> in their palms

> — EDNA KOVACS, SEPTEMBER 1992

As a teacher of "exceptional children" for the Portland Public Schools, I brought this activity to the children in my classroom at Shriners Hospital for Crippled Children. Students not only enjoyed creating poems, they also made collages by pasting and gluing the lichen, leaves, pine needles, moss, and twigs onto paper.... And for weeks, the hospital classroom resonated with smells from the forest! Create art projects. Listen to music! Explore your senses, and you will expand your awareness of who you are becoming.

As Annie Dillard points out in *An American Childhood,* "Children ten years old wake up and find themselves to have been here all along; is this sad? They wake like sleepwalkers, in full stride; they wake like people brought back from cardiac arrest or drowning…"

Listen to your own voice and share with others.

WARMING UP

EXPLORING THE SENSES
Smell, Taste, Touch, See, Hear

A poet with all her senses intact is Naomi Shihab Nye. When I read her poetry, I become magically transported into that moment of her poetic experience. It takes a special poet to be able to do this, and Naomi Shihab Nye is truly a master of her craft. This San Antonio poet has won the Lavan Award and is the widely published author and editor, of *This Same Sky, Yellow Glove, Different Ways to Pray,* and *Hugging the Jukebox,*

Read the following poem and become aware of the sensations that arise. Can you smell the coffee? Do you see the white cups, the family and guests gathered around the table? Can you imagine the voices of people talking in Arabic? Can you feel the breeze swaying through eucalyptus trees, perhaps, drying the clothes on the line? What is the poem saying without saying it all?

Image upon image is strung like beads on a necklace of poetic clarity. The reader genuinely becomes one of the guests — listening, watching, tasting, smelling, experiencing the vision of faith and hope that the traditional ritual of drinking Arabic coffee restores.

ARABIC COFFEE

It was never too strong for us:
make it blacker, Papa,
thick in the bottom,
tell again how the years will gather
in small white cups,
how luck will lie in a spot of grounds.
Leaning over the stove, he let it
boil to the top, and down again.
Two times. No sugar in his pot.
And the place where men and women
break off from one another
was not present in that room.
The hundred disappointments,
fire swallowing olive-wood beads

at the warehouse, and the dreams
tucked like pocket handkerchiefs
into each day, took their places
on the table, near the half-empty
dish of corn. And none was
more important than the others,
and all were guests. When
he carried the tray into the room,
high and balanced in his hands,
it was an offering to all of them,
stay, be seated, follow the talk
wherever it goes. The coffee was
the center of the flower.
Like clothes on a line saying
you will live long enough to wear me,
a motion of faith. There is this,
and there is more.

— NAOMI SHIHAB NYE

For me, Naomi Nye's "Arabic Coffee" brings back strong memories of an encounter I once had with two Arabic Bedouins who were returning back to their camp at dusk with a flock of goats in the foothills of the Carmel Mountains. We met by chance. I was nineteen years old at the time, and when they invited me into their tent for Arabic coffee, I accepted. *The coffee was the center of the flower.*

Close your eyes. Think back to your childhood and recollect smells and tastes, both good and bad. A campfire, the first spring rainfall, the ocean, spruce pitch, bus fumes, chlorine. Do you remember the first time you tasted sushi, fresh raspberries, spinach? Make a list of smells. Tastes. Associate sounds, textures, colors, light, feelings with them. Think about the experience. Sketch a first draft. Make it live for you in the moment.

For primary school children it may be helpful to begin brainstorming by drawing an idea wheel and/or writing a grocery list:

1. smells like…
2. tastes like…
3. sounds like…
4. looks like…
5. feels like…

Others may simply want to put on their writing goggles and dive immediately into that first draft.

The following are two poems that explore the senses on concrete and abstract levels.

LITTLE ROSE

Little Rose so sweet
you smell like a fantasy
When dew drops on
your petals.
It looks like crystals of
beauty.
You will grow till you're nice
as can be.
Sometimes your thorns hurt
and sting.
But you don't mean it.

— ANGIE HAGEL, GRADE 4, CORBETT GRADE SCHOOL, CORBETT, OREGON, FEBRUARY 1991

KALAHARI

As maize becomes dust
even thorn-scrub wither;
dry season is here.

Our pump has lost the will
to suck water from the dry-river sand.

Cockroaches crowd
beneath Degas' portrait of Mademoiselle Malo
hung high in my roundaval,
close to the thatched roof.

Grasses hum.
I skirt the dark places
scorpions, black mambas hide.

Flying termites wallow in the dirt,
burrow to coolness and mate
abandoning wings
to lay eggs.

Mealie meal, butter beans
and goat meat: rank
                        tough
                        salty
Nothing to drink.

The principal's wife
(whose right arm is fake)
draws me with her
to the tenant-farmers
and their cisterns on the hill.

Their hot tin sheds defy habitation;
evicted families coalesce on the steps,
their need for water
fallen from maize
to cattle
to children.

We step closer.

Suddenly, the farmers plead in Setswana
with the principal's wife.
She waves them away.

As children watch,
we dip our bottles
in the cistern
that reflects the cloudless sky.

Our bottles filled
we leave laughing
back to school
to teach.

— FRANCINE E. WALLS, LIBRARIAN, BELLEVUE COMMUNITY COLLEGE, BELLEVUE,
WASHINGTON

WARMING UP

DREAM PLACE

Close your eyes. Imagine a place you love. It may be the beach, a treehouse, your bedroom, the track, a swimming pool, a mosque, a place to hike, an imaginary landscape. What does your special place look like? Smell like? Feel like? Taste like? Sound like? Explore all your senses. You may want to cluster or list elements about your place as a prewriting activity. Once you've created your dream place, you can return there as often as you wish. It's a place where you can fly like a bird, swim like a fish, sing like a nightingale. It is an island only you can create, explore, and discover. Once you have, it will always be waiting.

MY SPECIAL TREE

In a
peaceful meadow,
Beside a winding, whispering brook
I lay beneath my special tree,
Fishing with a line and hook.
And clouds glide with a gentle breeze.
The air is becoming warmer,
But I'm cool beneath my special tree.
When the rain comes from the clouds,
And the sun goes away,
Because I'm beneath
my special tree
I still can have
a dry day.
Sometimes
inside of me
I feel lonely.
And some-
times just
sad, but
being beneath
my special tree

comforts me, and
calms me when I'm mad.

— ANA GONZALEZ, GRADE 6, BRUSH COLLEGE ELEMENTARY SCHOOL, SALEM, OREGON, SPRING 1991

DREAM PLACE

My utopia will be an island of peace among war. A place of refuge from the weather. A place for friends and me and mother.

My utopia will be contentness. It will not want to change. My utopia will have me & a Friend. It will have a computer.

But my friends can't be turned off and on. They aren't a machine, a toy, a plaything.

My friends will do all for me, and me for them. We will make our utopia for everlasting.

Utopia isn't HERE,
not there.
It's in my head,
under my hair.

— BEN KING, JUNIOR, JIM SAXTON'S AMERICAN LITERATURE CLASS, SANDY UNION HIGH SCHOOL, SANDY, OREGON, FEBRUARY 1989

THE SECRET GARDEN

One day I climbed the red brick wall to see what I could see. The flowers were all dying and the grass was brown, not green. There were dew drops streaming every place. It was like looking at a crying face. So one day I opened up the secret garden door, and it was not secret anymore. The flowers bloomed and the grass turned green, and now not only I have seen the garden that is known.

— JOCIE EDELSTEIN, GRADE 3, METROPOLITAN LEARNING CENTER CREATIVE WRITING CAMP, PORTLAND, OREGON, SUMMER 1992

After Jocie shared her poem aloud with the rest of the group, a quizzical look came over her face.

"It sounds like a poem," she began. "But it doesn't look like a poem, does it? How can I make this a poem?" she pondered, heaving a great sigh.

I asked Jocie to read the poem aloud again. I told her that wherever she paused to take a breath, I would make a slash (/), to indicate the natural line break. If you sing or play a wind instrument, you have natural pauses. Some are longer than others. Writing is as natural as breathing. Once you learn to trust in your own voice, you'll be able to see and hear where these line breaks want to occur. Always read your poems aloud.

I like to walk with mine — to hear and see them beyond the actual page. Once you've followed your own breath, you can then play with the way you'd like your poem to look like on the page. Will it be written in rhyme? Or free verse? Some poems naturally fall into couplets, tercets, quatrains…or freely flow as one continuous narrative.

As Lithuanian-born poet Czeslow Milosz puts it: "Poetry is a passionate pursuit of the real."

This is what Jocie's poem looked like upon revision.

THE SECRET GARDEN

One day I climbed the red brick wall
to see what I could see.
The flowers were all dying and the
grass was brown, not green.
There were dew drops streaming
every place! It was like
looking at a crying face.
So one day I opened the secret garden door,
and it was not secret anymore.
The flowers bloomed
and the grass turned green,
and now not only I have seen
the garden that is known.

MY PLACE

My place has lots of beautiful bushes and trees, thick green grass, a tree swing on one of the oaks. I'm barefoot and feel the rain falling down from the sky falling lightly to my clothes and body. This place has no boundaries and goes on forever and ever, up to the sky and down to the earth. This place can never let me down. It is there when I need it. I have loved this place forever and I always will. It is lovely and good. I wonder if this area could ever die? This place loves me, and me it.

The rain has stopped and sun now shines brightly from above the trees. The flowers blossom and grow ever forward up to the sky. This is my place and it is gorgeous. I ask myself how this place ever began and the answer is it was born when I was, it grows when I grow, it needs when I need, and it wonders when I wonder.

It is my imagination and it is the only place where I can let my whole self go and play in the thick emerald green grass. I run to the lake and jump in, always thinking of the big space where this scene fills my heart. This place is never too hot or cold. It is always warm and perfect, for it is in me.

— BETH ROGERS, GRADE 5, METROPOLITAN LEARNING CENTER CREATIVE WRITING CAMP, PORTLAND, OREGON, SUMMER 1992

MY DREAM PLACE

My dream place
is a basketball court
big and wide and you
and get autographs.

— RICKY KOTULSKI, GRADE 3, CORBETT GRADE SCHOOL, CORBETT, OREGON, FEBRUARY 1990

MY FUNNY LITTLE UNDER SEA DREAM PLACE

My dream place is
deep, deep in the sea,
Looking at the animals
look at me.

See the octopus
and all his legs,
Thinking he could
carry eight lunch bags.

Seeing all the fishes
looking like dishes,
Seeing whales that
swing their big tails.

That is where
I want to be.
Maybe I will,
I'll wait and see.

— SAM WILCOX, DRY HOLLOW ELEMENTARY SCHOOL, THE DALLES, OREGON, FEBRUARY 1991

WARMING UP

Imagination Hat

Have you ever noticed how clouds sometimes take on the shapes of bunny rabbits, mushrooms, flying fish? Take a look at the world around you. If you're wearing your imagination cap, you'll be able to suspend your belief in reality and revisualize windows, doors, pencils, clocks as other objects.

Several years ago, I had the opportunity to work with writer Jim Heynen through the Northwest Writing Institute at Lewis and Clark College's "Writers at Home in Oregon Libraries" program. Jim is the author of *A Suitable Church, The Man Who Kept Cigars In His Cap, One Hundred Over 100,* and most recently *The One-Room Schoolhouse.* We were working with a group of third and fourth graders in Port Orford, Oregon.

As a prewriting activity, Jim tossed his cap into the air and began: "A hat is not a hat — what else does it look like?" and he instructed the students to put on their imaginary imagination caps.

"A hat is not a hat. It's a flying saucer!" one child bellowed.

"And if I open it up and start picking strawberries, what is it then?" Jim asked.

"It's a basket for picking strawberries."

What else does a triangle look like? The number 8? The letter V? A triangle isn't a triangle, it's a slice of pizza with olives, mushrooms, and green peppers on it. The number 8 isn't the number 8, it's a snowman. Turn it around sideways and it's a pair of eyeglasses. The letter V isn't the letter V, it's the wings of a bird.

A good writer is attuned to his or her senses. Open your eyes. Tell us what you see. Discover the world of images.

A piece of paper
isn't a piece of paper.
It's a surf board that's white.

— BRYAN

An alligator isn't an alligator.
It's a suitcase
with eyes.

— CHRIS

The ceiling isn't a ceiling.
It's a flat pancake
that's square.

— MARCY

A rainbow isn't a rainbow
it's a horseshoe
in a sky.

— RENA

A person isn't a person.
It's a whole bunch
of designs.

— BROOKE

A flag isn't a flag.
It's a red, white, and blue whale
hanging in the air.

— FAWN

— FIRST GRADE STUDENTS IN MRS. CONTOIS' CLASS, BRUSH COLLEGE ELEMENTARY, SALEM, OREGON, 1991

A clock isn't a clock. It's a grapefruit that tells time. Got the idea? Now you try it!

WARMING UP

SHRINKING FOR DETAILS

My students from all walks of life have enjoyed shrinking to the size of a pea — closing their eyes and using all of their senses to write from the perspective of a fly, a ketchup bottle at McDonald's, a squirrel.

In the Spring of 1993, I taught a creative writing workshop to families (ages 9–adult) at Cedar Hills Recreation Center in Portland, Oregon. One of the mothers, Elisa Weger, a mother and teacher, was fascinated by the way my clustering assignment — which asked students to draw an idea wheel around a color — took the writers into a realm of global/lateral thinking, while shrinking for details — becoming a speck of dust, a molecule, a raindrop — can be a highly scientific/analytic journey.

The following are some of Elisa Weger's suggestions for ways teachers can link shrinking across the curriculum: Close your eyes and travel to your "bird's eye" world.

1. Life Science:
   A study of the digestive system in the human body. Imagine you are a piece of food — tell about your journey.

2. Botany:
   A study of the parts of a rose. Be an aphid that crawls the length the flower, learning the names for the parts of the flower and their functions.

3. Oceanography/Zoology:
   Exploring tidepools. Be a small sea creature in a tidepool — a starfish, sea anemone, barnacle or jellyfish. What floats by? What is the interdependence of sea creatures?

Variations: Be a gnat in a rainforest
              a fly in a jungle
              a mosquito in a forest
              a bee on a skyscraper
              an ant in a kitchen pantry

4. Physics and Auto Mechanics:
   Nuts and bolts.
   You have become a drop of grease inside an engine. Describe what you see!

Variations: Be a screw inside a television set, a computer, or an air conditioner.

These are just a few of the possibilities. Topics may be explored orally as well as through the written word.

As Elisa Weger has suggested, shrinking for details is a useful vehicle for writing, research, and oral expression. Through my years of teaching experience, I have observed that shrinking may not only be extended across the curriculum, it also adapts itself to all the modes of writing — be they persuasive, expository, narrative, descriptive, or imaginative.

Think about it! In the world of the arts, for example, one may become an instrument, a paintbrush, an arabesque. We could dive into the area of music alone and fill the pages of this manuscript with ideas for themes and variations: imagine you are a key on the piano, a bow to a cello, a string on a viola, or an f#.

Explore all your senses. Listen and celebrate!

~·~· **ALARM** ·~·~

She always hits
my head 8:00
in the
morning

I scream her to
get up, but
she never does

And then, she
blames me for
being late.

Oh, what a hard
life I have

Mina

— Minako Nishimori, Readings in English & American Literature class, Linfield College, McMinnville, Oregon, Fall 1992

WARMING UP

SOUNDS OF POETRY
Silent, Loud, Eternal

Poet, essayist, folklorist, and storyteller Kim Stafford offers this suggestion and the example that follows: Tell three silent, three loud, and three eternal things.

A LIST TO MEMORIZE

Silent things are a deaf person
talking with her hands,
a hollow tree when the coon
is gone into the moonlight,
a person after they have died
singing to their friends.

Loud things are a rattlesnake's explosion
by your foot, people laughing at you
when you say a secret by mistake, your own
great heart in the middle of a drum.

Things that last forever are
the color black, the taste
of salt, and the word
"good-by."

— *KIM STAFFORD*

Did you know that much good writing comes from the ability to listen? As a prewriting activity, take a walk around the block and record the sounds that you hear: a robin singing, the wind rustling through leaves, a dog barking, the sound of your own footsteps. Or close your eyes and mentally record the sounds you hear rush past you in a matter of seconds: traffic, a telephone ringing, the tea kettle whistling....

This is a highly successful individual and group poetry and lyrical prose writing activity for people of all ages.

This warm-up activity may also be approached from a thematic perspective. Students may tell three silent, three loud, and three eternal things about a person, place, or thing.

Given the theme, "Endangered Species," the following poem was written by a group of fourth grade students in Mr. Misetich's class during a Young Audiences of Oregon "Writing as Discovery" workshop that I taught at Harvey Scott Elementary School in Portland, Oregon, in January 1993.

THE GOLDEN EAGLE

1.
an eagle
flying over the canyon

flying up and down
over the rainbow

the mountains
quietly in their place

2.
the eagle
hears a gunshot

a storm
lightning coming down

the rapids of the river
flowing

3.
the eagle
never dies

the eagle's golden wings
never rest

the sound of the wilderness
roaring

Experiment with line breaks, punctuation, stanzas that work with phrasing.

MY DAD

Silent

is the sound of his hugging me
It's the huffing and puffing of riding
  his bike up a hill
Of his sleeping and resting

Loud

is the sound of a drill at my Dad's
  work
It's the ringing of the phone, Bart asking
  him about his notes
of screaming to get one of the guys
  for the phone

Eternal

is the love for him from me
It's the happiness of knowing he
still loves me
of the place in my heart I hold for
  him

— LIANNE KELLEY, AGE 11, METROPOLITAN LEARNING CENTER CREATIVE WRITING SUMMER
CAMP, OREGON, JULY 1992

A to Z

From
African Drum Song
to
Blues,
Ghazal
to
Haiku,
Villanelle
to
the Zoo

A to Z

ACROSTICS
Spelling Poems

What's your name? How do you celebrate holidays? What are your favorite sports? What's life like in a rainforest? Acrostics can be about anything!

A lmonds & Peanuts
L emons
I ce cream too
S oup and
S paghetti
A RE ALL GOOD FOR YOU!

— ALISSA SILVER, AGE 10, METROPOLITAN LEARNING CENTER CREATIVE WRITING CAMP,
PORTLAND, OREGON, SUMMER 1992

RAINFOREST

R is for rabbits to keep hopping
a is for apple trees to keep growing
i is for islands — green, yellow and brown
n is for nuts — walnuts and peanuts.
f is for fish wild and free,
o is for orangutans that swing from trees
r is for the rap-a-tat-tat of the woodpeckers
e is for elephants and their babies too
s is for snakes that slither
t is for tiger and turtles.

— FIRST GRADE CLASS, NELLIE MUIR SCHOOL, WOODBURN, OREGON, FEBRUARY 1992

A to Z

AFRICAN DRUM SONG

Master drummer Obo Addy was born into a fetish house in Ghana, West Africa, where drumming, singing and ritual ceremonies were a part of everyday life. As the son of a Wonche priest and medicine man, he learned the traditional drumming of the Ga culture at an early age. He is committed to passing along his traditions with people throughout the world.

GOME is music from Accra that includes history. When the British were in Ghana, they took men to Cameroon to work for them. Some of the carpenters among them built frame drums out of wood and created a dance. Gome tells both sad and happy tales.

Some of the songs are in Pidgin English that the Ghanaians used to communicate with the British. For example: "Shippi fall down, sailor wan go shaw" means the ship was sinking and the sailor wanted to swim ashore. "Me don't know trobo, me don know" — is about the age old adage: If you don't listen to your parents, you can get yourself into trouble.

Listen to Obo Addy and Okropong's "Traditional Music of Ghana" — available on CD or cassette from The Homowa Foundation, 2915 NE 15th Avenue., Portland, Oregon, 97212.

Clap rhythms.

Learn the lyrics of "Gome" by heart.

Create your own sacred songs, dances.

Make masks.

Working independently or in small groups, create your own African Drum Songs!

For students with verbal language disabilities such as autism and cerebral palsy, a code can be created on the drum to express words, ideas, images, much like a language board.

This activity may be successfully linked to a social studies unit on Africa. Through research and preparation, students may wish to create an African village — portraying the social organization, rituals and ceremonies of the Ga culture, for example.

ENGLISH LYRICS TO GOME

Shippi fall down, sailor wan go shaw
Shippi fall down, sailor wan go shaw

Shippi fall down, sailor wan go shaw
Shippi fall down, sailor wan go shaw
Shippi fall down, sailor wan go shaw
Shippi fall down, sailor wan go shaw

Shippi fall down, sailor wan go shaw
Shippi fall down, sailor wan go shaw

Shippi fall down, sailor wan go shaw
Shippi fall down, sailor wan go shaw

Me don know trobo, me don know
Me don know trobo, me don know,
Fatha telli me I don hear, me don know,
Mother telli me I don hear, me don know trobo

Me don know trobo, me don know
Me don know trobo, me don know,
Fatha telli me I don hear, me don know,
Mother telli me I don hear, me don know trobo

Me do know trobo, me don know
Me don know trobo, me don know, trobo trobo
Fatha telli me I don hear, me don know,
Mother telli me I don hear, me don know trobo

— OBO ADDY

A to Z

ALLITERATION
Sounds of Poetry

Choose a letter of the alphabet and see how many words you can make using that sound.

For example:

moon monkeys make marvelous magic at midnight

or

big bees bulldoze buildings on Broadway

Put that sound in the beginning, middle, and ending of words and create a poem!

BRACES

steel
stupendous
stressful
strenuating
stupid feeling
strange looking
sore causing
summer heat producers
short-wave receivers
sometimes shock absorbers
sorrowful zinc bits
soundly keeping out
slowly put on
suddenly taken off
straightening me out

— VICTOR HOFFER, GRADE 8, MT. ANGEL UPPER ELEMENTARY SCHOOL, MT. ANGEL, OREGON, FEBRUARY 1991

A to Z

ANDALUSIAN CANTE JONDO
("Deep Song")
Traditional Gypsy Chants

In his introduction to Lorca's *Poem of the Deep Song*, Carlos Bauer writes:

In 1921, Frederico Garcia Lorca wrote his first major work, Poem of the Deep Song. In it, the twenty-three-year old poet crystallized the themes that would run through all his great works: love, death, and alienation. For Lorca, these poems explore the essential character of the Andalusian soul.

Traditionally, Andalusian people expressed their feelings through deep song or cante jondo. The four major types of song that comprise cante jondo are the Gypsy Siguiriya, the Solea, the Saeta, and the Petenera.

Lorca believed the Gypsy Siguiriya to be the "genuine, perfect prototype" of deep song, the one that most preserved its deepest origins. Siguiriyas are sung with a rising emotional tension, interrupted by sudden cries of anguish (the ay!), and unexpected silences. The song ends with a gradual fading away of both voice and guitar. The lyrics express life's most tragic dramas, its intensest moments. Because of its extreme emotional demands, mastering the siguiriya is the apex of the singer's quest.

The following two examples of Gypsy Siguiriya, are Lorca's exploration into this Gypsy-Andalusian-flamenco cosmos: the poems are images provoked by deep song, the emotions produced within the listener. Yet while Lorca strove to capture essences, his poems express the same themes and world view as cante jondo, and they recreate a tapestry of Andalusia's mystery and pain, the true Andalusia, the one lying just beneath its sundrenched landscape. What we have here is not some tourist Andalusia filled with happy-go-lucky Gypsies and picturesque whitewashed villages. Lorca has given us a corner of the earth that is populated by dead lovers and lost, wandering souls; where the blade of

a knife flashing in the black, the desolate cry, and a millennium of tears
expose Andalusia's almost erotic passion for life, and for death.

— CARLOS BAUER

EL GRITO	THE CRY

La elipse de un grito
va de monte
a monte.

Desde los olivos,
será un arco iris negro
sobre la noche azul.

¡Ay!

Como un arco de viola,
el grito ha hecho vibrar
largas cuerdas del viento.

¡Ay!

(Las gentes de las cuevas
asoman sus velones.)

¡Ay!

The ellipse of a cry
travels from mountains
to mountain.

From the olive trees
it appears as a black
rainbow upon the blue night.

Ay!

Like the bow of a viola,
the cry has made the long
strings of the wind vibrate.

Ay!

(The folks from the caves
stick out their oil lamps.)

Ay!

EL PASO DE LA SIGUIRIYA

THE PASSING STAGE OF THE SIGUIRIYA

Entre mariposas negras,
va una muchacha morena
junto a una blanca serpiente
de niebla.

Tierra de luz
cielo de tierra.

Va encadenada al temblor
de un ritmo que nunca llega;
tiene el corazón de plata
y un puñal en la diestra.

¿Adónde vas, siguiriya,
con un ritmo sin cabezá?
¿Que luna recogerá
tu dolor de cal y adelfa?

Tierra de luz,
cielo de tierra.

Among black butterflies
goes a dark-haired girl
next to a white serpent
of mist.

Earth of light,
sky of earth.

She is chained to the tremor
of a never arriving rhythm;
she has a heart of silver
and a dagger in her right hand.

Where are you going, siguiriya,
with such a headless rhythm?
What moon'll gather up your pain
of whitewash and oleander?

Earth of light,
sky of earth.

— FREDERICO GARCIA LORCA

In the tradition of cante jondo, what are your deepest songs? You may follow the forms of the two examples by Lorca. Above all, be honest. Prepare the world to share who you are.

You and your students should listen to gypsy music, take a field trip to a Hispanic neighborhood, watch a video about Spain. You may wish to create skits and dances.

A to Z

BALLAD
A Narrative Poem

According to a definition from Babette Deutch's *Poetry Handbook*, a ballad is a short simple narrative poem. The folk ballad was anonymous, composed to be sung, and altered as it was repeated from generation to generation without being written down. The ballad presents a romantic theme, impersonally treated, and is characterized by the simplicity of the language, the repetition of epithets and phrases, the casual handling of rhyme, the liberties allowed by stress prosody. The folk ballad which flourished in fifteenth-century England and Scotland has lived on into our own time in the Southern Appalachians and other secluded areas.

While the mediaeval ballad has its counterpart in our cowboy ballads, the literary ballad is a skilled imitation of the anonymous popular form.

The following literary ballad was written by Johann Wolfgang von Goethe and craftily translated by Wilma M. Erwin. Goethe was considered Germany's greatest lyric genius. Born on August 28, 1749, in Frankfurt am Main, his greatest work is "Faust," which is known all over the world. He died in Weimar, Germany, on March 22, 1832. "Der Erlenkoenig," written in 1776, is one of his earlier writings. It has a ballad quality to it and is written with a rhyme scheme of aa, bb, cc, dd, etc. There are eight stanzas to "Der Erlenkoenig"—and if you can figure out the rest of the rhyme scheme, go to the head of the class.

THE ERLKING

Who's riding so late through the night?
It is the father with his child.
He holds the boy safe in his arms,
He holds him secure; he keeps him warm.

"My son, why do you hide your face in fright?"
"Father, can't you see Erlking by our side?

The Erlking with shining crown and train?"
"My son, it's only the mist on the plain."

"Come, dear child, come with me, do!
Beautiful games I will play with you.
Many colored flowers grow by the shore;
My mother has garments of gold galore."

"My father, my father, do you not hear
what Erlking is now promising in my ear?"
"My child, be calm, stay calm as can be;
it's the wind rustling dried leaves in the trees."

"Will you go, dear child, will you go there with me?
My daughters will treat you like royalty!
My daughters will lead their nightly dances.
They'll rock you to sleep with loving glances."

"My father, my father, do you not see
the Erlking has brought his daughters for me."
"My son, my son, I see it all right.
The aged gray willows are deceiving your sight."

"I love you, I'm enthralled by your charm,
and if you're not willing, I'll do you great harm."
"My father, my father, he's touching me now!
Erlking has brought great pain to my brow."

The father gallops, in horror half wild;
he holds in his arms the groaning child.
He reaches the courtyard with toil with dread:
the child in his arms is motionless — dead.

— JOHANN WOLFGANG VON GOETHE, TRANSLATED BY WILMA M. ERWIN

DER ERLENKOENIG

Wer reitet so spaet durch Nacht und Wind?
Es ist der Vater mit seinem Kind;
Er hat den Knaben wohl im Arm,
Er fasst ihn sicher, er haelt ihn warm.

„Mein Sohn, was birgst du so bang dein Gesicht?" —
„Siehst Vater du den Erlkoenig nicht?
Den Erlkoenig mit Kron und Schweif?" —
„Mein Sohn, es ist ein Nebelstreif."

„Du liebes Kind, komm, geh mit mir!
Gar schoene Spiele spiel' ich mit dir;
Manch' bunte Blumen sind an dem Strand,
Meine Mutter hat manch' guelden Gewand."

„Mein Vater, mein Vater und hoer est du nicht,
Was Erlenkoenig mir leise verspricht?" —
„Sei ruhig, bleibe ruhig, mein Kind:
In dueran Blattern saeuselt der Wind."

„Willst feiner Knabe, du mit mir gehen?
Meine Toechter sollen dich warten schoen;
Meine Toechter fuehren den naechtlichen Reih'n
Und wiegen und tanzen und singen dich ein."

„Mein Vater, mein Vater, und siehst du nicht dort
Erlenkeonigs Toechter am duestern Ort?" —
„Mein Sohn, mein Sohn ich seh' es genau"
Es scheinen die alten Weiden so grau."

„Ich liebe dich, mich retzt deine schoene Gestalt:
Und bist du nicht wilig, so brauch' ich Gewalt." —
„Mein vater, mein vater, jetzt faast er mich an!
Erlenkoenig hat mir ein Leids getan!" —

Dem Vater grauset's, er reitet geschwind,
Er haelt in den Armen das aechzende Kind,
Erreicht den Hof mir Mueh und Not;
In seinen Armen das Kind war tot.

— JOHANN WOLFGANG VON GOETHE, TRANSLATED BY WILMA M. ERWIN

What are your popular folk songs and ballads? Create sea shanties, mur-
der ballads, cow-country songs, historical songs, and love songs using the
ballad form.

A to Z

BIOGRAPHY
Sharing Cultures

The following exercises were contributed by poet and teacher Sister Helena Brand of Marylhurst, Oregon, who was recently named Poet of the Year by the Oregon State Fair.

What is your story?

1. Who are you?

2. What is your name? What does your name tell about yourself? What does it tell others about yourself?

3. If you could give yourself a different name, what would it be? What does this new name mean? What would it tell about yourself?

4. Where were you born? Where did you come from? City? Town?

5. Where did your grandparents come from? Mother's side? Father's side?

6. What is your nationality?

7. What language(s) do you speak at home?

8. What kind of neighborhood did you grow up in? Ethnic/American?

9. How did you celebrate birthdays?

10. How did you celebrate holidays?

11. Describe a memorable family meal.

12. Who are your favorite relatives?

13. What are your favorite foods?

14. Have you any ethnic traits that you are proud of? Conceal? Why?

BIOGRAPHY

Two students. One reads information 1–14; then the other reads the same. Compare and contrast.

POETRY

Students take turns reading their first lines, second lines, and so on. This makes for a poem which is a source for sharing cultures.

Consider the following "Who are you?" poem by one of the greatest poets in American literature, Emily Dickinson (1830–86). She composed over one thousand unique lyrics dealing with nature, love, religion, immortality, and death. Only seven of her pieces were published during her lifetime.

> I'm Nobody! Who are you?
> Are you — Nobody — Too?
> Then there's a pair of us?
> Don't tell! they'd advertise — you know!
>
> How dreary — to be — Somebody!
> How public — like a Frog —
> To tell one's name — the livelong June —
> To an admiring Bog!
>
> — EMILY DICKINSON

A to Z

JAMMIN' ON THE BLUES
After Langston Hughes

Black American poet Langston Hughes (1902–67) was born in Joplin, Missouri. He was a major figure in the "Harlem Renaissance." Besides poetry, he wrote plays, children's books, and novels often portrayed urban black life.

> *The Negro folk songs, known as the Blues, unlike the Spirituals, have a strict poetic pattern: one long line, repeated, and a third line to rhyme with the first two. Sometimes the second line in repetition is slightly changed and sometimes, but very seldom, it is omitted. Unlike the Spirituals, the Blues are not group songs. When sung under natural circumstances, they are usually sung by one man or one woman alone. Whereas the Spirituals are often songs about escaping from trouble, going to heaven and living happily ever after, the Blues are songs about being in the midst of trouble, friendless, hungry, disappointed in love, right here on earth. The mood of the Blues is almost always despondency, but when they are sung people laugh.*

> — Excerpted from The Dreamkeeper by Langston Hughes

Jammin' on the blues, Langston Hughes uses a less traditional approach to express his "Dressed Up" blues.

DRESSED UP

I had ma clothes cleaned
Just like new.
I put 'em on but
I still feels blue.

I bought a new hat,
Sho is fine,
But I wish I had back that
Old gal o' mine.

I got new shoes —
They don't hurt ma feet,
But I ain't got nobody
for to call me sweet.

— *Langston Hughes*

At a Writing Festival in Banks, Oregon, I gave seventh and eighth graders the blues as a poetry writing assignment. One seventh grader wrote: "I'm grounded/I'm pounded/I've got the no Nintendo Blues!/"

A long time friend and blues musician, Curtis Robertson, who plays bass guitar with Lou Rawls, shares his L.A. blues, which he says was written while driving.

L.A. BLUES

The smog it makes my eyes water,
    The stress makes my heart race,
       One day I'm gonna pack up
Pack my bags and leave this place.
         LA.........LA.........

This city of fallen angels by the sea
       One day I'm gonna pack up
Gonna pack my things and leave.

— *Curtis Robertson, Los Angeles, California, August 1993*

Write some blues. You may even want to compose a melody and sing them aloud.

A to Z

CALENDAR POETRY
From the Czech Republic

The following poem, "August," is excerpted from Czech poet Karel Toman's sequence of calendar poems titled *The Months*, translated by Jirina Fuchs. Karel Toman (1877–1946), who published his first verses in the nineteenth century, was a poet of personal lyric and social protest; an alienated and disinherited wanderer from his native land who returned, in the maturity of age, to the themes, scenes, and traditions of his home — that cultural continuity that runs like a golden thread throughout Czech literature.

AUGUST

The murmur of grain fields
fragrant like bread
permeates my garden closed to the world.
The peaceful song of the harvest
walks through the fields
and under the blazing sun
man wipes from his brow
the sweat of finished labor.

From afar
I hear the screeching of barn-gates,
the sound of the gnashing teeth.
An invisible robbing hand
leans against a weapon
waiting.
And yet I keep quiet.
I shall not cry out into the silences.

Above us, keeping guard,
sunflowers, the clocks of our solitudes,
bow their heads.

— *KAREL TOMAN*

Create a calendar by writing poems about each month. Combine art work with the poems. Work in teams. Your calendars will make lovely gifts and classroom decorations! You may want to photocopy or print the calendars so they can be shared with a wider audience.

A to Z

CALLIGRAMME
Picture Writing From
the 20th Century French Poet,
Guillaume Apollinaire

In *Sleeping on the Wing*, Koch & Farrell write:

> *The French poet Guillaume Apollinaire lived and wrote at the end of the nineteenth and beginning of the twentieth century. He was killed in World War I. His lifetime corresponded with the beginning of modern times, of the modern world, the world of automobiles, airplanes, electricity, and modern cities....And Apollinaire lived in Paris, the most beautiful city of the world, the city that was the center of art and science and thought, where it seemed that everything that mattered was going on. More than other poets, Apollinaire seemed to feel, and was able to express in his poems, the spirit and the excitement of his time. His poems are full of praise for the beauty of modern things — airport hangars, newspapers, billboards, new industrial streets — and, like life in a modern city, the poems are often fragmented and rapidly changing. He was moved by the beauty of airplanes as other poets were moved by the beauty of roses. He was also moved by roses. What he found in the new century, and in modern Paris, was not something harsh and mechanical and unpoetic but a new simplicity, variety, and beauty.*
>
> *New kinds of experience not only gives the poets and other artists new subjects for their work but also often inspire them to find new forms for it, new ways of writing, different ways of painting. The excitement about the modern did this in all the arts. The Cubist painters, for example, whom Apollinaire was friends with and whose work he very much admired, painted pictures like none that he had ever seen before — showing things from different viewpoints at once, and full of angles and flatness, more like a modern street than, say, a meadow. Like Cubist paintings, Apollinaire's work was new and un-*

conventional. There's no punctuation; when there is rhyme, it is so light and flat it is hardly noticeable, although sometimes it seems that the rhyme has, in fact, inspired the line; the style is often very conversational and plain; the poem often shifts from one place and time and subject to another. Apollinaire's most obviously radical modern invention in poetry is the form he calls calligramme (the word seems related to Oriental picture-writing, calligraphy, and also to telegram). Instead of the usual shape of poetry, the poem has a shape determined by its subject. The letters of a love poem form the outline of a heart; the letters of a poem about rain fall like raindrops from the top to the bottom of the page. Such poems don't read like other poems, they don't even look like them.

"It's Raining" is a rain of words, a rain of letters of words, and also a rain of memories and feelings. These lines of rain are curved a little bit to the right, as if blown by a gentle spring breeze. The rain makes Apollinaire think of the past, of the women he has known. It may be the soft sound of the rain that makes him think of their voices. Then he thinks of "marvelous meetings," probably meetings with the women he has loved. Then, probably looking at the sky, he sees the "crooked clouds" and hears thunder, and its roar reminds him of the roar of cities he has been in, with their noises of traffic, of people, of machines. All things are gone now, only memories brought back by the rain. The rain binds him to the sky, where the rain begins; and to the past, where his memories begin. It binds him also to the present and to the earth, where he really is now, alone and in the rain. And the falling letters of the poem (and the raindrops too) look like a rope or a chain.

A sudden change in the weather often brings back memories. The first snow, the first warm day, can seem to bring back other snows and other warm days when you were younger and things were different. It can seem, as in Apollinaire's calligramme, that the memories and the weather are all part of the same thing.

To write a calligramme, begin with the shape of something and let that shape suggest to you what to write. In Apollinaire's calligramme, he doesn't write about rain in general; he writes about a particular rainy day, when he has certain feelings and certain memories. Try making your poem particular in that way. For instance, if your poem is in the shape of clouds, let the clouds be clouds of a certain day when you looked at them and thought and said and did certain things, and let your poem be about those clouds and that day. If the poem is in the shape of a telephone, maybe you could write about a certain conver-

sation. If it's in the shape of a window, it might be a particular window in your house that you always look out of, waiting or thinking. A nice thing that happens in writing a calligramme is that the shape of the poem and the subject of the poem become mixed up and seem the same. You may want to write several.

— FROM SLEEPING ON THE WING BY KENNETH KOCH & KATE FARRELL

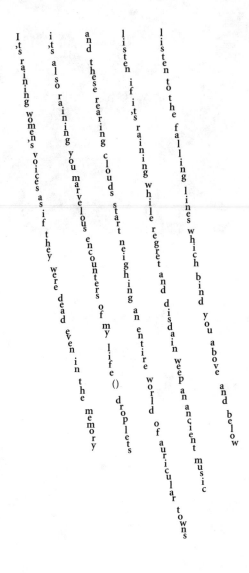

— GUILLAUME APOLLINAIRE

— *EMIKO SEO, LINFIELD COLLEGE, FALL 1992*

A to Z

CINQUAIN
A Quintet, From the French,
With a Five-line Syllabic Pattern

A cinquain poem pattern is: two syllables
four syllables
six syllables
eight syllables
two syllables

Choose a theme. Write about Nature, Animals, Sports, Friends, Places. Link cinquain writing across the curriculum — from Math to Social Studies, Science to Spanish....

The following are cinquains written by fourth graders at Riley Creek Elementary School in Sally Prince's "Writing With Words Workshop" in Spring 1991. Sally is a Poet-in-the-Schools and journalist in Port Orford, Oregon.

FREE FROGS
frisky leapers
screaming, soaking, swimming
very difficult to catch one
JUMPER

— ZAC SMITH

AMIGOS
BUENO, HUEGAH
CHEVO, RAMON, PEPE
MEACUERDO DE ELLOS
AMIGOS

— JUAN

BALLOON

pop, break, fly, soar
falling, fascinating
flying in the sky like a bird
floater

— *Jason*

RAINDROPS

wet, water, slick
dropping, dumping, dripping
comes down steady for a long time
patter

— *Elliot Neal*

BEACHES

sandy, windy
fishing, flying, crashing
a pretty place with land and sea
Seashores

— *Carl Hoogesteger*

GOLD BEACH

Peaceful, small, fun
befriending, beautiful
knowing everybody is good
Home town

— *Kyle Ringer*

DRONE BEES

busy workers
big, busy, buzzing bugs
nature's architects of beauty
Insects

— *Isaiah Lara*

SERPENT

slithery, quick
snaring, catching, stealing
always slithering in patches
Viper

— *Aaron Smith*

RIVERS

beautiful, clear
gurgling, rushing, chasing
swift or slow they're fun to play in
creeks, streams

— *Amy Lyn Woolley*

KITTEN

funny, cute, sweet
playing, running, meowing
Is there when you are really sad
Kitty

— *Crystal S.*

A to Z
RHYMED COUPLETS
Two-line Stanzas of Rhymed Verse

Rhymed couplets are two lines of verse, usually in the same metre, that form a unit, such as the example by Alexander Pope.

ENGRAVED ON THE COLLAR OF A DOG, WHICH I GAVE TO HIS ROYAL HIGHNESS

I am his Highness' dog at Kew;
Pray tell me, sir, whose dog are you?

Make a rhymed couplet calendar and illustrate it with paintings or photographs. Write rhymed couplet poems about summer, fall, winter, and spring. Here are two examples.

MONTHS

The month of January
is colder than February

In January they have snow
In February they have a fashion show

In the month of March
people like to march

In the month of April
lots of mothers name their daughters Mapril

In the month of May
lots of kids want it to stay

In the month of June
kids dig with a spoon

In the month of July
birds like to fly

In the month of August
people wipe off dust

The month of September
is hotter than October

At the end of November
people start to say BRRR

In the month of December
lots of women begin to wear fur.

— KATHY SAVELIEFF, GRADE 7, MT. ANGEL UPPER ELEMENTARY SCHOOL, MT. ANGEL, OREGON, FEBRUARY 1991

OFF TO THE MEADOW IN SPRING

I made a pot of plenty
I add a drop of honey

I drop some dijon mustard
I'll serve it with some lemon custard

Off to the meadow I'll meet my friend there
You can have some toast with honey but don't get it in your hair

I'll skip and skip and bring my dog along
On my way I'll sing a delightful song

Back again, back again, I once said
I'll skip home and go right to bed!

— SIERRA STEENSON, GRADE 4, CORBETT GRADE SCHOOL, CORBETT, OREGON, MARCH 1991

A to Z
COWBOY & COWGIRL POETRY
"Give me a home where the buffalo roam…"

Once, on a seven-hour bus ride from Portland to Enterprise, Oregon, I met retired teacher, cowboy poet, carpenter, and horse trainer Bud Paasch from Caldwell, Idaho. As we rode through the Blue Mountains, he recited his poetry. I don't think I've ever enjoyed a long bus ride as much as I did that one. And I will never forget the last two lines of a poem he recited: "Don't ever step on a cowboy's toes/or he'll forever change the way you sit!"

The following two poems from Hal Cannon's anthology *Cowboy Poetry: A Gathering*, reflect the honest, tough, hard-bitten spirit behind this literature.

Nyle A. Henderson's "'Bueno,' Which in Spanish Means Good," is a humorous ballad; Vern Mortensen's "Range Cow in Winter" is a lyrical elegy. Henderson breaks horses and recites poems out of his ranch in Hotchkiss, Colorado. Mortensen has ranched and herded sheep in the country around his home in Parowan, Utah. But you don't have to be a cowgirl or a cowboy to write poetry of this kind. You do need to go beyond the television image, however, by reading and discussing the rich lore of cowboy poetry.

If you visit a rodeo, stick around and listen to the talk. If the range isn't your destination, try writing poetry about your vocation — waitress, student, bus driver, or imagine having the life of a dog! Students can also write about parents' vocations or something they'd like to be! Be sure to include the slang and special language that is indigenous to the particular culture.

"BUENO," WHICH IN SPANISH MEANS GOOD

Stick around now and I'll tell ya one more,
This happened to me when I was with the Figure 4.
I'd been out doctorin' cows all afternoon,
And it was just about dark on the last day of June.
The day it seemed had gone awful slow,

I'd been workin' with a Mexican named Emelio.
He was fair with a rope and not too bad with a horse,
So our biggest problem was our language, of course.

I explained what we was doin' as best as I could,
He just smiled and said, "Bueno," which in Spanish means
    good.
We found a lame cow down by the spring,
So I figured it was time we do our thing.

I says to Emelio, "What would you say
If we doctor this cow and then call it a day?"
Now my horse was tired and needed a rest,
So I decided to put ol' Emelio to the test.

I told him to rope her and I hoped that he would.
He just smiled and said, "Bueno," which in Spanish means
    good.
I circled around to run her out through the trees,
And she took off like a feather that's caught in a breeze.

And then there went Emelio on a dead run,
I just stood there and thought, now this might be fun.
She dove down through the brush like an old freight train,
Right behind her was Emelio, he didn't complain.

After awhile a yell came up out of the draw.
So I rode down to the clearing and guess what I saw?
He'd caught her and stopped and dallied up tight,
But you should have seen Emelio, man what a sight!

His shirt was all tore and he'd lost his hat.
He wasn't feelin' too happy, I'll bet you on that.
I was still laughin' about the time that he'd had,
And then I saw that Emelio was gettin' kinda mad.

I gave her a shot so he could turn her loose,
Then Emelio decided it was time to cook my goose.
He undid his rope and that set her free,
She was plum on the fight and a-lookin' at me.

I beat it for the brush and I'm tellin' ya now,
I didn't want nothin' to do with that mean ol' cow.
I climbed as high as I could in an old oak tree,
And then I saw Emelio was a laughin' at me.

But he wouldn't come and chase her off like he should,
He just smiled and said, "Bueno," which in Spanish means
good.

— NYLE A. HENDERSON

RANGE COW IN WINTER

Have you listened still on a desert hill
    At the close of the bitter day,
When the orange sun in wispy clouds
    Was set in a greenish haze?
In a cold white world of deepening drifts
    That cover the land like a pall,
Then the plaintive bawl of a hungry cow
    Is the loneliest sound of all!

Have you listened still on a desert hill
    When the world was cold and drear,
When the tinkling bells of a herd of sheep
    Was the nearest sound you'd hear,
And the haunting notes of a lone coyote whose
    Evening's hunting howl
Rose wild and clear in the cold blue night,
    And was answered by the hoot of an owl?

But when the scanty grass lies covered deep
    By the snow that lies like a pall,
Then the plaintive bawl of a hungry cow
    Is the loneliest sound of all!

— VERN MORTENSEN

This narrative poem about life on the farm in Corbett, Oregon, is told from the animals' points of view.

THE TALKING BARNYARD

"Good morning," said the horse to the
    sheep.
"Good morn' to you too, my dear," as
    he crunched in a bucket of oats.
"Hello," said the cow with the bell on
    his neck. "How's the weather?"

"Aw, quite nice," said the horse.
"And, "Coo," went the birds up, out of
    the way.
"Here comes our master with some hay."
"Oats, with a side order and some bread
    on the way."
"Aw," said the horse.
"Good day," said them all and went away.

— JOANNIE LOEHR, GRADE 5, CORBETT GRADE SCHOOL, FEBRUARY 1991

A to Z

DADAIST POETRY
Chance Meetings of Meaningful Words

Here's an idea suggested by Tristan Tzara in *Chanson Dad*. To make a Dadaist poem, take a newspaper. Take a pair of scissors. Choose an article as long as you are planning to make your poem. Cut out the article. Then cut out each of the words that make up this article and put them in a bag. Shake it gently. Then take out the scraps one after the other. In the order in which they left the bag, copy conscientiously. The poem will be like you. And here you are a writer, infinitely original!

CIVILIZATION

New construction fails dancing evolution.
A measure, mixture, open on canceled culture.
Side victory in the dark, close hall the event for.
Repressive could, and blessings begins.
On project up, disguise move is the set,
in not to really stop, in of a place to eat.
To moths tying women, bias of liberal slips.
invite to, after pounds for up, those lose.
Against extra up, at a media and gears.
Remain.

— WILLIAM WILES, FRESHMAN, LINFIELD COLLEGE, FALL 1992

DISCOVER MIND DAY

Man shalt calling into romantic
birthday covet thou driven long pain
agony overcoming the memories bed weight
neighbor's love. extraordinary taste handle
plane steamy dead might hate country free
wife about not plots another preppy
other popcorn help America better sleep

— SARAH LAMERS, FRESHMAN, LINFIELD COLLEGE, FALL 1992

Discover mind Day.

by Sarah Lamers
Linfield College

MAN SHALT CALLING into romantic

BIRTHDAY COVET THOU DRIVEN long PAIN

AGONY overcoming the memories bed weight

NEIGHBORS LOVE. extraordinary taste Handle

plane steamy dead might Hate country FREE

WIFE about NOT plots another PREPPY

other Popcorn help America better sleep

A to Z

EPISTLE
A Letter-poem

An epistle is a letter in verse, such as Ezra Pound's poem below. Pound (1888–1972) was one of the most influential and controversial figures in 20th century poetry. He influenced many major poets such as T.S. Eliot and James Joyce, and is noted for his translations from many languages. Here Pound has emulated the ancient Chinese poet Li Po's "A Song of Ch'ang-kan."

THE RIVER MERCHANT'S WIFE: A LETTER

>While my hair was still cut straight across my forehead
>I played about the front gate, pulling flowers.
>You came by on bamboo stilts, playing horse,
>You walked about my seat, playing with blue plums.
>And we went on living in the village of Chokan:
>Two small people, without dislike or suspicion.
>
>At fourteen I married My Lord you.
>I never laughed, being bashful.
>Lowering my head, I looked at the wall.
>Called to, a thousand times, I never looked back.
>
>At fifteen I stopped scowling,
>I desired my dust to be mingled with yours
>Forever and forever and forever.
>Why should I climb the lookout?
>
>At sixteen you departed,
>You went into far Ku-to-en, by the river of swirling eddies,
>And you have been gone five months.
>The monkeys make sorrowful noise overhead.
>
>You dragged your feet when you went out.
>By the gate now, the moss is grown, the different mosses,
>Too deep to clean them away!

The leaves fall early this autumn, in wind.
The paired butterflies are already yellow with August
Over the grass in the West garden;
They hurt me. I grow older.
If you are coming down through the narrows of the river Kiang,
Please let me know beforehand,
And I will come out to meet you
　　As far as far as Cho-fu-Sa.

— EZRA POUND

Write a letter poem to a friend, a loved one, or to yourself. Ask questions. Use metaphor and imagery. Primary school children may wish to write a letter poem to their perfect pet, a favorite animal, or a storybook animal. Go to the zoo, your local library, or your own backyard and research.

The following epistles to animals were written by students during an Artist-in-Education residency I taught.

Dear Great Dane,
How did you get so big?
Why do they call you G.D.?
Why do people call you
handsome?
　　　　　Goodbye,
　　　　　Angel

Dear Komodo Dragon,
Why do you live
in the desert?
What's Africa look like?
Do they have teepees?
　　　　　Good-bye!
　　　　　Nick

— THIRD GRADE STUDENTS, LYNNETTE LANG'S CLASS, BRUSH COLLEGE ELEMENTARY SCHOOL, SALEM, OREGON, SPRING 1991

A to Z
FUGUE
Writing With Music
A Theme and Variations

According to Apel & Daniel's *Harvard Brief Dictionary of Music,* a fugue is a polyphonic composition based on a theme (subject) that is stated at the beginning in one voice part alone, being taken up (imitated) by the other voice or voices in close succession, and reappearing throughout the piece.

As poetry or prose, the fugue may be approached as a theme and variations. Listening to compositions by great fugal composers, such as Bach and Shostakovich, you will hear how the theme is represented by a straight line, while other melodic materials may be represented by wavy lines.

Fugues often have episodes, where the subject is not being stated in any voice part. In music, short empty spaces are meant to illustrate the fact that often the voice parts have a rest, particularly before a new theme.

Writing with music is one way to approach this form. I like to ask my students to cluster a color and/or a feeling. A theme and variations may evolve the way a musical composition would. Alternating between tonic and dominant keys, tone color, and paying attention to all the details between subject and answer challenges the poet to explore the possibilities of language, text and subtext.

A poem that illustrates the way the fugal form can be transposed into poetry is Diane Wakoski's well-crafted, polyphonic poem "Blue Monday."

BLUE MONDAY

Blue of the heaps of beads poured into her breasts
and clacking together in her elbows;
blue of the silk
that covers lily-town at night;
blue of her teeth
that bite cold toast

and shatter on the streets;
blue of the dyed flower petals with gold stamens
hanging like tongues
over the fence of her dress
at the opera/opals clasped under her lips
and the moon breaking over her head a
gush of blood-red lizards.

Blue Monday. Monday at 3:00 and
Monday at 5. Monday at 7:30 and
Monday at 10:00. Monday passed under the rippling
California fountain. Monday alone
a shark in the cold blue waters.

> You are dead: wound round like a paisley shawl.
> I cannot shake you out of the sheets. Your name
> is still wedged in every corner of the sofa.

> Monday is the first day of the week,
> and I think of you all week.
> I beg Monday not to come
> so that I will not think of you all week.

You paint my body blue. On the balcony
in the soft muddy night, you paint me
with bat wings and the crystal
the crystal
the crystal
the crystal in your arms cuts away
the night, folds back ebony whale skin
and my face, the blue of new rifles,
and my neck, the blue of Egypt,
and my breasts, the blue of sand,
and my arms, bass-blue,
and my stomach, arsenic;

there is electricity dripping from me like cream;
there is love dripping from me I cannot use — like acacia or
jacaranda — fallen blue and gold flowers, crushed into the street.
> Love passed me in a blue business suit
> and fedora.
> His glass cane, hollow and filled with
> sharks and whales...

He wore black
patent leather shoes
and had a mustache. His hair was so black
it was almost blue.

"Love," I said.
"I beg your pardon," he said.
"Mr. Love," I said.
"I beg your pardon," he said.

So I saw there was no use bothering him on the street

Love passed me on the street in a blue
business suit. He was a banker
I could tell.

So blue trains rush by in my sleep.
Blue herons fly overhead.
Blue paint cracks in my
arteries and sends titanium
floating into my bones.
Blue liquid pours down
my poisoned throat and blue veins
rip open my breast. Blue daggers tip
and are juggled on my palms.
Blue death lives in my fingernails.

If I could sing one last song
with water bubbling through my lips
I would sing with my throat torn open,
the blue jugular spouting that black shadow pulse,
and on my lips
I would balance volcanic rock
emptied out of my veins. At last
my children strained out
of my body. At last my blood
solidified and tumbling into the ocean.
It is blue.
It is blue.
It is blue.

— *Diane Wakoski*

A more concrete approach to the fugue/theme and variations is to ask primary students to choose a color, feeling, person, place, or thing — and make a list to walk through in verse.

For example: Blue is...blueberries. Now put yourself into the poem. Include experiences that you associate with being blue into the poem — although they don't necessarily have to be blue in reality.

/Blue are the blueberries I pick/beneath a
blue sky/with my blue dog on Sauvie's Island/

The following examples of a concrete listing approach to this form were written at Brush College Elementary School during an Artists-in-Education Creative Writing residency that I taught in 1991 and at Silver Star Elementary School during a workshop I presented in 1992.

PINK

Eating my pink apple
under the pink stars
on the pink grass
Looking at the pink water
with my pink hair
with my pink bear
Looking at the pink leaves
eating pink popcorn
I feel happy.

— Marina, grade 3, Brush College Elementary School, Salem, Oregon, April 1991

WHITE

White is
    a soft breeze
    or a snowflake on my nose
White is
    a wedding,
    a shower of love.
White is
    soft, not too rough,
    white is a beautiful color.

— Regina Sevshek, grade 3, Silver Star Elementary School, Vancouver,
Washington, March 1992

Students may express their hopes, fears, loves, and desires by approaching feelings in a theme and variation format.

The following poem was written in one of my college writing classes at Linfield College during a weekly freewriting class.

I HATE

You know when cars cut you off in the street
and it really makes you mad? I hate that.
I hate when cars drive slow in the fast lane
and you get in a gridlock with cars in the slow
lane.

I hate dogs that jump up on you and
get your clothes muddy.
I hate people who borrow your things without asking.
I hate when adults exercise power on you
just because they're adults.

I hate when you get pulled over for having a
defective blinker and the cop accuses you
of drinking. I hate when people you know
get diseases. I hate when people don't respect you.
I hate when people don't believe your stories.

I hate when pizza burns the roof of your mouth.
I hate when I don't get any letters.
I hate when I lose my keys. I really hate my car
'cuz it always breaks down. I hate spending money
on things I don't want but need.

I hate people who think they are above people.
I hate when people are negative. Ha! Ha! Ha!
I hate when people deny having a drinking or
drug problem. I also hate when people deny having
an eating disorder problem.

But I do love my life
and I love to get my feelings out.

— *Alex Benson, freshman, Linfield College, September 1993*

And this Fugue in gold was written by a third grade teacher during a creative writing in-service I offered to teachers while doing an Artists-in-Education residency in 1992.

POT OF GOLD

The rainbow's colors
        in various hues
From pastel shades
        to brilliant and true,
When woven together —
        strengthen each other,
Yet keep their own
        identity known.
This harmonious blend
        at the rainbow's end,
Shines in this room —
        disguised as children.
A treasure so dear,
        each one as they are —
Will glow, and grow brighter,
        together, this year.

— MRS. ORTEGA, TEACHER, COLONEL WRIGHT ELEMENTARY SCHOOL, THE DALLES, OREGON

A to Z

GHAZAL
Linked Verse
From What is Now Afghanistan

The ghazal is a form of poetry that has several characteristics in common with the Japanese renga (linked verse written in 3-line, 2-line links with as many as 100 links around a hokku, or theme).

—Ghazals are written in five couplets.
—As in renga, construction is associative. One idea breeds another.
—Narrative is not required but may exist. The whole ghazal may encompass one image or it may fly away.
—No effort is made to regulate the length of line or syllables.

As to the origin of the ghazal, it is defined in Islamic literature as a genre of lyric poetry, generally short and graceful in form.

— ADAPTED FROM CAROL ATKINS' ESSAY IN LYNX, AUTUMN 1990

The following ghazal was written by the American and international students in my Readings and Writings in Literature class at Linfield College, McMinnville, Oregon, October 1992.

Silence is winter
when snow gently falls

Thunder is loud
living in a cloud

Something that lasts forever
is the air that we breathe

A quiet flute
soft, like the wind

Softly singing voices
fill the night.

— CONTRIBUTORS: HEATHYR BALSIGER, SHIGEYUKI KATSUUMI, AKI NAKIMITSU, KAORI
NATSUGARI, RIE SAKAMOTO, HISAKO SEKIGUCHI, EMIKO SEO, AYA SHABATA, YUI SUZUKI,
JOE WHEELER, HIROKO YAMADA, MISAKO YAMAGUCHI, KIMI TERASAKA, MINAKO
NISHIMORI, TARO SHIINA, TOMOKO UCHIDA

The following ghazal from Ghalib (1797–1869) is interpreted here from
the Urdu by Oregon's best loved poet, the late William Stafford.

GHAZAL 1

Only Love has brought us to the world:
Beauty finds itself, and we are found.

All time, all places, call — here, not here:
no mirror finds the truth but in itself.

To know — what do we know? To worship —
emptiness takes us into that craving.

Any trace, glimpse, whatever flickers —
that's all we have, known or not known.

Held by the word, targeted here in openness,
Earth receives the sky bent forever in greeting.

— GHALIB

ABOUT GHALIB AND THE GHAZAL

*The seven decades of Ghalib's life (1797–1869) were not a very
auspicious time for the writing of poetry for anyone who lived in the
city of Delhi. The British conquest of India was completed during
those decades, the fabric of the entire civilization came loose, and the
city of Delhi became a major focal point for countless traumatic cri-
ses. Ghalib was not, in the modern sense, a political poet — not political, in other words, in the sense of a commitment to strategies of
resistance. Yet, surrounded by constant carnage, Ghalib wrote a poetry primarily of losses and consequent grief.... In sensibility, it is a
poetry somewhat like Wallace Stevens': meditative, full of reverbera-
tions, couched in a language at once sparkling and fastidious, and
testifying to a sensibility whose primary virtue was endurance in a
world that was growing for him, as for many others of his time and
civilization, increasingly unbearable. The journey from nothingness*

to a totally human affirmation which is the essential growth of a poet of that tradition — beyond time, beyond the merely spatial relations — was achieved in his case with a necessary and austere urgency related, finally, to the experience of having been possessed. He is a tragic poet.

Like Persian, Urdu is very much a language of abstractions. In this sense, it is very difficult to translate from the Urdu into English. The movement in Urdu poetry is always away from concreteness. Meaning is not stated; it is signified. Urdu has only the shoddiest tradition of dramatic or descriptive poetry. The main tradition is one of highly condensed, reflective verse, with abundance and variety of lyrical effects, verbal complexity, and metaphorical abstraction…Ghalib demands patience. He expects that you will read his couplets together, that you will let these couplets sink into your consciousness, and will let themselves reveal themselves to you gradually, over the years. he expects that you will read these couplets as impressions of a man who sought wholeness at a time when wholeness was difficult…Ghalib was a man who wrote poetry because poetry was necessary.

— Excerpted from Ghazals of Ghalib, Versions of the Urdu, Aijaz Ahmad, Editor

Working on ghazals as a class or group is a highly successful writing activity. You can list couplets on the blackboard or computer and use a renga-like approach.

A to Z
HAIKU
From Japan
Celebrating Nature in 3 Short
Lines

Haiku were originally fragments of a longer poetic form called waka, which consisted of 31 syllables grouped 5-7-5-7-7. During the Heian period (794–1191) the waka was split into two independent sections, one of 17 syllables (5-7-5) and one of 14 syllables (7-7), each section linked to its neighbors by the association of words or ideas. In the Kamakura period that followed (1192–1392) the renga form was expanded from two parts to long chains, and from a double link to as many as 100 links. In expression of the eastern philosophy of "selflessness," links were written by different authors working together. It was only from the fifteenth century on that haiku began to be liberated from the constraints of the renga and recognized as an independent literary form.

It took the genius of Basho, another two hundred years later, to create from the modest 17 syllables of a haiku the masterpieces we associate with the form. Moreover, he promulgated an esthetics. A haiku has shiori, a "tender feeling," and hosomi, a "slenderness in its expression" — nothing excessive. It has sabi, "dry hardness." Sabi derives from sabishi, which means "lonely or solitary," a feeling Oriental artists and poets, who see life as a small part of the universe, attach importance to. A haiku also has what Daisetz T. Suzuki called wabi, a taste for the quiet and homely: "wabi is to be satisfied with a little bit, a room of two or three tatami (mats) [a small room], like the log cabin of Thoreau, and with a dish of vegetables pickled in the neighboring fields, and perhaps to be listening to the pattering of a gentle spring rainfall."

...To write a haiku the poet "gets inside an object, experiences the object's life and feels its feelings. You learn of the pine from the pine, of the bamboo from the bamboo": empathy — except that in the East, empathy is extended to all things, not just sentient beings. A haiku poet gets inside a piece of wood, feels its "woodness." The poet "becomes" a flower, tree, water. A haiku does not describe. Description introduces a division between poet and experience, stands outside them. In haiku, poet and experience become one. All is related to all. Haiku are quiet celebrations of nature written in three short lines of 5-7-5 syllables.

the old pond —
a frog jumps in
plunk!

— BASHO

furu ike ya
old pond —
kawazu tobikomu
frog jumps in
mizu no oto
water [poss.] sound

snail,
climb Mt. Fuji —
oh slowly

— ISSA

katatsumuri
snail
sorosoro nobore
slowly slowly climb
Fuji no yama
Fuji [poss.] Mount

> — EXCERPTED FROM HIAG AKMAJIAN'S SNOW FALLING FROM A BAMBOO LEAF: THE ART OF HAIKU.

Write haiku in all seasons. In fall, for example, pick up a leaf and it will tell you what to say. The following haiku was written by a freshman from Hawaii in one of my college writing courses in 1993. When he shared his haiku aloud, the "AHS" echoed across the room — and he was asked to read it again and again.

With a gust of wind
I could be thrown from my home —
life is precious.

> — MARK KURISU, FRESHMAN AT LINFIELD COLLEGE, FROM WAHIAWA, HAWAII, OCTOBER 1993

The following haiku was written during an Artists-in-Education residency I taught in 1990.

turtles sit around
slow, green, one step at a time —
their homes upon their backs.

— First grade students, South Sherman Elementary School, Grass Valley, Oregon, April 1990

Take a field trip to your local Japanese garden. Walk in the forest, mountains, desert — by the sea. Be in nature and write haiku.

A to Z

HOLOCAUST POETRY
In Remembrance of the
Persecution and Extermination of
European Jews in Nazi Germany

The following are excerpts of essays, letters, journal entries, and poetry written by liberators, poets, and survivors of the Holocaust which occurred between 1933–1945, when over 6 million Jews were murdered under the power of Adolf Hitler.

Holocaust poetry addresses the unique horror of the Nazi Holocaust. A variety of genres may be explored such as acrostics, essays, ghazals, journals, quatrains, or villanelles.

CONFRONTING THE HOLOCAUST

Not all victims were Jews,
But all Jews were victims.

The Holocaust was an event contemporaneous in large part with World War II — but separate from it.
The Holocaust begins with the Jews as targets; but it takes in all humanity as victim. For, once the Holocaust began — once the plan took hold — values and morality fell victim just as surely as did lives.
Since the Holocaust, we need not theorize about human potential for evil: we need to face up to it as fact. We need to see that progress cannot be measured in technology alone; history has shown that technology's successes can still go hand-in-hand with morality's failures.
From the Holocaust, we begin to understand the dangers of all forms of discrimination, prejudice, and bigotry: hatreds, which, in their extreme forms, can lead to the world evils of mass slaughter and genocide — and, on the personal level, can endanger our ethical being. From the Holocaust, we can learn the way evil can become commonplace and acceptable so long as change is gradual — so that no

one takes a stand until it is too late.

From the Holocaust, we can examine all the roles we humans play: victim or executioner; oppressor or liberator; collaborator or bystander; rescuer; witness. From the Holocaust, we are reminded that humans can exhibit both depravity and heroism. The victims of Nazi persecution demonstrated tremendous spiritual heroism of those who risked their lives to save others. From the Holocaust, we must remember the depths to which humanity might sink; but then we must remember, as well, the heights to which we might aspire.

— ELIE WIESEL, SURVIVOR OF AUSCHWITZ AND WINNER OF THE NOBEL PEACE PRIZE IN 1986

THE LIBERATORS

The American Army moved east across Germany toward Berlin in early 1945. As the troops progressed they discovered scores of concentration camps. Soldiers of all ranks were amazed and horrified at what they saw.

The things I saw beggar description... The visual evidence and verbal testimony of starvation, cruelty, and bestiality were so overpowering as to leave me a bit sick. In one room, where there were piled up twenty or thirty naked men killed by starvation, George Patton would not even enter. He said he would get sick if he did so. I made the visit deliberately, in order to be in a position to give first-hand evidence of these things, if ever, in the future, there develops a tendency to charge these allegations merely to "propaganda."

— GENERAL EISENHOWER'S LETTER TO CHIEF OF STAFF GEORGE MARSHALL, APRIL 12, 1945

When we saw
the ovens,
we were
silent.
Not a word
spoken, not
a single
expression.
Not, *Oh Jesus,*
not, *What is
this?* Not,
*What have we
done?*

— AMERICAN LIBERATOR

And there were
bones. God,
there were bones, all
over the place,
wherever you
stepped there
were little
bits of bones.

— *American Liberator*

We, the rescued
From whose hollow bones death had begun to whittle his
      flutes,
And on whose sinews he had already stroked his bow —
Our bodies continue to lament
With their mutilated music.
We, the rescued,
The nooses wound for our necks still dangle
before us in the blue air —
Hourglasses still fill without dripping blood
We, the rescued,
The worms of fear still feed on us.
Our constellation is buried in dust…
We, the rescued,
Beg you:
Show us your sun, but gradually.
Lead us from star to star, step by step.
Be gentle to teach us to live again.
Lest the song of a bird,
Or a pail being filled at the well,
let our badly sealed pain burst forth again
and carry us away —
We beg you:
Do not show us an angry dog, not yet —
It could be, it could be
That we dissolve into dust —
Dissolve into dust before your eyes.

— *Nobel Prize-winning poet, Nelly Sachs*

One day when we came back from work, we saw three gallows rearing up in the assembly place, three black crows. Roll call. SS all around us, machine guns trained: the traditional ceremony. Three victims in chains — and one of them, the little servant, the sad-eyed angel.

The SS seemed more preoccupied, more disturbed than usual. To hang a young boy in front of thousands of spectators was no light matter. The head of the camp read the verdict. All eyes were on the child. He was lividly pale, almost calm, biting his lips. The gallows threw its shadow over him.

This time the Lagerkapo refused to act as executioner. The SS replaced him.

The three victims mounted together onto the chairs.

The three necks were placed at the same moment within the nooses.

"Long live liberty!" cried two adults.

But the child was silent.

"Where is God? Where is He?" someone behind me asked.

At a sign from the head of the camp, the three chairs tipped over.

Total silence throughout the camp. On the horizon, the sun was setting.

"Bare your heads!" yelled the head of the camp. His voice was raucous. We were weeping.

"Cover your heads!"

Then the march past began. The two adults were no longer alive. Their tongues hung swollen, blue-tinged. But the third rope was still moving, being so light, the child was still alive...

For more than half an hour he stayed there, struggling between life and death, dying in slow agony under our eyes. And we had to look at him full in the face. He was still alive when I passed in front of him. His tongue was still red, his eyes not yet glazed.

Behind me I heard the same men asking:

"Where is He? Here He is — He is hanging here on the gallows..."

That night the soup tasted of corpses.

— "NIGHT," BY ELIE WIESEL, 1986

We could never
understand the
townspeople not
knowing about
the camps. They

swore they never
knew. They told
us there were
camps in the
United States.
But there was
no way you couldn't
know. No matter
which way the wind
blew, you could
smell it.

— *American Liberator*

I don't know that
we were angry
We were too numb
for that. We were
drained, iced over,
frozen. It was
just too much. We
couldn't take it
in. We couldn't
have any human
feelings. That
came later, when
I woke for a month
of nights, screaming.

— *American Liberator*

*Though Jewish, profoundly Jewish in nature, the Holocaust has
universal implications, and I believe, we believe, that the memory of
what was done may shield us in the future.*

— *Elie Wiesel, survivor*

This little car
came out of Dachau.
I picked it up
in the street.
Some child had
brought it. My

wife has painted
it black. She
painted the little
wheels red. I did
not see any children
in Dachau — alive.
We always have
a Christmas tree
in our house. And
underneath the tree
we always have a
garden. We always
have skiers, farm
animals, a little
village and that
car from Dachau.
It's our family's
tradition.

— AMERICAN LIBERATOR

— EXCERPTED FROM DAYS OF REMEMBRANCE OF THE VICTIMS OF THE HOLOCAUST, A
   DEPARTMENT OF DEFENSE GUIDE FOR COMMEMORATIVE OBSERVANCE, OFFICE OF THE
   SECRETARY OF DEFENSE, THE PENTAGON, WASHINGTON, DC

From the Lodz Ghetto comes the song "Winter 1942 — Lodz Ghetto"
written by Miriam Harel. According to Gila Flam in *Singing for Survival*:

> *Miriam Harel's ghetto songs, interwoven with her life story, are
> examples of personal expression as well as a means for survival dur-
> ing times of great psychological stress. The ghetto songs were com-
> posed, mainly in Polish, between 1941 and 1945. In order to preserve
> the songs she reconstructed them in Italy after her liberation in 1945,
> while awaiting permission to immigrate to Israel.*
>
> *Miriam often asks herself why she survived. Her answer is that she
> was the "right" age: In Lodz, she was young enough to believe that
> there would be an end to suffering and was buoyed by the hope. By the
> time she arrived in Auschwitz, she was old and robust enough in ap-
> pearance to pass "the selection" and so she was spared. After enduring
> these ordeals, she realized that she would be one of the few survivors
> in her family to tell her story.*

VINTER 1942 — GETTO LODZ
(WINTER 1942 — LODZ GHETTO)

Verse 1:
Father and mother in the graveyard.
My brother sent away.
My sister is sick, a walking cripple,
I am weak from hunger.

Verse 2:
In the house there is no food at all,
No bread, not even carrots could we find.
I have already forgotten how to chew.
Empty, vacant is the table.

Verse 3:
It's cold, my fingers are frozen,
I have only slippers on my feet,
At night I cry from my great hunger,
My life is dark and miserable.

Verse 4:
There is no mercy in heaven,
Satan stands there and laughs,
He laughs at the orphans and widow
Locked up in the Lodz ghetto.

Verse 5:
I walk around like an old man,
My eyes are wet and red,
The sky is dark and cold,
And tomorrow death will come.

— MIRIAM HAREL, FROM GILA FLAM'S SINGING FOR SURVIVAL

As a high school senior at Corvallis High School in Corvallis, Oregon, Manuel Roth tied for Division II's 1st Place Award in The Fourth Annual Sala Krysek Holocaust Writing Competition, sponsored by the Oregon Holocaust Resource Center in Portland, Oregon in April 1993. The poem is in two voices:

HOLOCAUST

| cold | laughs |
| my hands rough | burn |

i look out my window
white grey black
prison
food
i am hungry
my bones are visible
beneath my skin
hell
mother
i need to find
you where is father
i fear
them
hair
falling out
need food weak need
help why do they
hate
where
are you when i
need you god please
no more hate
war
barbed
wire cutting
hurts to look at us
hanging dead
here
why
us why do
they come after us
beat us
pain
help
us need food
why do we fear
them so
much
why
do they
rape women and

and torture me
why are we so
weak we cannot
stop
this
hell is killing
us so quickly
yet days
drag
pain
always with me
he hums at me
when i think
i'm
alone
i sit and wonder
why he always laughs
and hits me
hard
floor
beneath us crawls
with bugs rats get more
food than
us
rat
i see you
do you think you can
have my
food
i eat
you rat if i
could catch you
i would
eat
toes
frozen together
maybe broken off
like his but mine
i cannot see
grey
the room is dark

girls scream
hurt
are
we such
bad people that god
does this to
us
father
i am a jew
why does
he who

i wait they
walk outside
not
looking our
hands held out we
plead for food
they
spit
on us we
can do nothing because
fear does nothing

— *Manuel Edan Roth*

In remembrance of the Holocaust, research and write specific responses. For further information, contact your local library, temple, or Holocaust Resource Center.

A to Z

I WAS THE LAST PERSON ON EARTH AND THERE WAS A KNOCK AT THE DOOR…
Science Fiction/Fantasy/Mystery/ Adventure

Imagine that you wake up one morning, only to find that you are the last person on Earth and there's a knock at the door!

Before writing, you or your students may want to outline the following:

1. Character(s)
2. Setting
3. Plot
4. Action/Dialogue
5. Organic Conflict
6. Theme

But that's not the only approach. Some writers prefer the characters to take the pen and they just follows along. Other writers make use of brainstorming techniques — clustering, listing, shrinking for details. Explore any genre and use any method that works best.

The following is the first chapter of a fantasy written at a Creative Writing Summer Camp I taught to 9–14 year olds through the Metropolitan Learning Center's Community Schools Program, Portland, Oregon, in 1992.

I WAS THE LAST PERSON ON EARTH AND THERE WAS A KNOCK AT THE DOOR…

I was the last person on Earth and I heard a knock at the door. I walked over to the door and looked through the peep-hole, and since it was okay, I opened the door.

When I opened the door, there was a person standing there. It was me. I said, "What are you doing here?"

The other person exclaimed, "I am the last person on Earth and I came to my house."

"This is not your house!" I yelled.

"It's my house, and there is only one of me and I know that for a fact."

"You must be from another world because... Well, just because."

"I am a nice, calm person. I like apple pie and — "

As the other person babbled to herself, I thought to myself, "This person is crazy and she thinks she is me."

Just then, I snapped and slammed the door on her face and heard a loud OUCH! I ran through the house locking and closing all the windows and doors. I picked up the phone and listened to the dial tone and realized there was no one to call because I was the last person on Earth, even though there was a person at the back door pounding and yelling at me.

I went to my room and turned on the music as loud as it would go, so I couldn't hear the person or whatever was in my backyard yelling at me.

Soon I got bored and turned off the music and sat down to watch TV. But once again there was no TV because I was the last person on Earth.

I went outside to look for the person. I couldn't find her so I got into my Dad's Corvette and drove. I didn't know what I was doing because I had never driven a car before, but I knew I couldn't get caught because I was the last person on Earth.

— TRACY LOVENSTEIN, GRADE 7, TROUTDALE, OREGON, JULY 1992

A to Z

JOURNAL WRITING

Through her own perspective as a black woman, Beryl Hammonds' journal *I am Not a Dark-Skinned White-Girl!!* invites any reader or writer to explore and share ways for seeking understanding from the inside out as well as becoming more aware of one's own views on cultural diversity.

What you feel matters. Read, reflect, and respond to the following affirmations from Beryl Hammonds' journal. You may want to illustrate your writings with pen and ink drawings, photographs, watercolors, or create a collage with newspaper and magazine captions.

From the journal:

> *from nigger to colored*
> *from negro to black,*
> *from black to afro-american,*
> *from afro-american to a person of color,*
> *from a person of color to african-american*
> *to refining who you are by first*
> *defining who you are not…*
>
> *I am Not a Dark-Skinned White-Girl!!*
>
> *Culture without heritage is like pearls without a string to make them into a necklace.*
>
> *Inferiority is a state of mind, treatment as inferior is racist.*
>
> *Learn the hazards of racism. It will keep you from becoming the very thing you hate.*
>
> *I had to give myself permission to cry to give myself permission to stop.*
>
> *It is virtually impossible to feel your self-worth when you are hungry.*

I am hungry...for respect. As I grew older I learned to feed myself.

Some days I feel like both sculptor and clay.

— Excerpted from Beryl Hammonds' I am Not a Dark-Skinned White-Girl!!, A Distinct Production, PO Box 1764, Vancouver, Washington, 98668

The following is a student response to Beryl Hammonds' journal by Cherina Knight, a freshman in one of my college writing classes.

Reading through Beryl Hammonds' I am Not a Dark-Skinned White Girl!! and not being a dark-skinned white girl, reminded me of my senior year in high school second period leadership class.

A group of students, myself included, set out to do something never done before in the small town of Canby, Oregon. It was a very hard, but a very good and brave thing for us to do. We founded the first Cultural Diversity organization: Unite.

Our motto was: "Free your mind, Unite your soul." We plastered this and other quotes from great leaders such as Martin Luther King Jr., up in the halls of our schools. We also had assemblies and speakers teaching the importance of all cultures in our society today.

For our first year I think we were well received. But, in small town Canby, Unite is going to take a lot of growth.

— Cherina D. Knight, freshman, Linfield College, October 1993

A to Z

KOREAN HYANNGA
"Native Songs"

As Latin was the written language of Italy until the nineteenth century, so classical Chinese was the primary written language of Korea until the fifteenth. In the absence of a writing system of native origin, an ingenious system was devised by the Silla people to transcribe their spoken language using Chinese logographs. Some graphs were used for their original meaning, and some were borrowed for their phonetic values to transcribe particles and inflections. The system came to be used from the sixth century on; and it was through it that the extant old Korean poems, or hyannga, were preserved.

Most old Korean poems were written or rather sung by members of the hwarang and by the Buddhist monks. The hwarang was an indigenous institution which recruited men of ability for national service and educated them as soldiers, statesmen, and poets. Monks provided the guiding spirit in this training.

Some hyannga gained their resonance through verbal felicity and symbolism. The "Ode to Knight Kip'a," for example, begins with a symbolic equation between the moon that pursues the white clouds and the speaker seeing the depths of his friend's mind, and concludes with a correspondence between the knight and the pine that "scorns frost, ignores snow." Like the pine tree, encompassing the past, present, and future through its roots, branches, and leaves, the knight represents the principle of growth and order: an emblem of continuing society and culture.

From early days on, poetry and music played an important part in the daily lives of Korean people. Unfortunately, little of the earliest flowering Korean poetry has survived, owing to oral transmission and the lack of a unified writing system. The lyrics of the surviving hyannga are for the most part Buddhist in inspiration and content, reflecting the contemporary trends in Silla and early Koryo Buddhism.

Hyannga ("native songs") is the term for the twenty-five extant

*Old Korean poems. Of the three variants, the most polished and popu-
lar consisted of two stanzas of four lines plus a conclusion of two lines.*

— Excerpted from The Anthology of Korean Literature, edited by Peter H. Lee

ODE TO KNIGHT KIP'A

The moon that pushes her way
Through the thicket of clouds,
Is she not pursuing
The white clouds?

Knight Kip'a once stood by the water,
Reflecting his face in the blue.
Henceforth I shall seek and gather
Among pebbles the depth of his mind.

Knight, you are the towering pine
That scorns frost, ignores snow.

— Master Ch'ungdam (fl. 742–765)

Listening to Korean p'ansori music, which is Korea's epic vocal art and
instrumental music, I assigned the hyannga as a writing assignment to a
group of Korean and Japanese students who were enrolled in my Introduction to College Writing class at Linfield College. The following are two responses. Notice the use of symbolism and imagery in these rich, lyrical odes.

ODE TO MT. NAMSAN

The long history
which it has witnessed
since the dawn of Chosun, is heard
riding in the wind.

There is a refined art that
ancient scholars enjoyed.
There are reliant spirits that
the white-clad folk have kept in their hearts.

Mt. Namsan, you whisper to me
that I shall tread the right path.

— Chong Si Won, Seoul, Korea, May 1993

ODE

Time changes everything into memories.
Time leaves you just memories.
You will miss these memories.
But don't look back on these memories too long.
Memory is an illusion.
Memory is a shadow.
The shadow might not do anything for you.
You should not feel sad for the shadow.
Time is a big river.
You should get on the ship with your dream.

— *Takako Ishida, Maebashi, Gumma, Japan, May 1993*

A to Z
LIMERICKS
"Will you come up to Limerick?"

The limerick is a sometimes bawdy, but popular form of humorous verse of three long and two short lines rhyming aabba, as in this anonymous example:

> There once was a boy of Bagdad,
> An inquisitive sort of a lad.
> He said, "I will see
> if the sting has a bee."
> And he very soon found out that it had.

The first time I attempted to teach limericks was during an Artists-in-Education residency in Corbett, Oregon. One afternoon, the students had a two-hour assembly, which left me time to explore nearby Multnomah Falls. Climbing the path above the Falls, I noticed a sign which read:

> Stepping off the trail is no joke
> Because you might end up in poison oak!

This sounded like the beginning of a limerick to me. When I returned to Corbett Grade School, I brought this phrase to a class of rowdy fifth graders on a Friday afternoon. We completed the limerick as follows.

> So you better beware
> You'd better take care
> Or else in a tub you'll end up in a soak!

Other limericks the students composed included variations on the strict form. Students even explored their own line breaks.

SUSHI

There was once a man who liked one dish
because he loved that fish.
It was called sushi
and it was very mushy
but the fish wanted one last wish.

— GENO O'NEIL, GRADE 5, CORBETT GRADE SCHOOL, FEBRUARY 1991

DEAR, DEAR LORANCE

There
once
was
a horse
named
Lorance
who
tried
to
impress
dear
Florance
He
asked
for
a
dance
but
tripped
on
his
pants
and
that
was
the
end
of
dear
Lorance

— BROOKE KINNEY, GRADE 5, CORBETT GRADE SCHOOL, FEBRUARY 1991

A to Z

LINKED VERSE FROM KOREA

From ancient to modern times, linked verse has engaged people from all walks of life into exploring a collective point of view on one topic. Linked verse writing may extend across the curriculum. It also may be linked to the arts, such as responding to a piece of music, and is a vital method for delving into current events.

Five young fifteenth century scholars at the Hall of Worthies — Song Sam-mun, Yi Kae, Shin Suk-chu, Pak P'aeng-nyon, and Yi Sok-hyong — were granted a leave of absence to study at the Chin'gwan monastery on Mount Samgak, where they composed a number of linked verses.

UPON LISTENING TO THE FLUTE (1442)

Where does it come from, the sound of a flute,
At midnight on a blue-green peak?   *Song Sam-mun*

Shaking the moonlight, it rings high,
Borne by the wind, it carries far.   *Yi Kae*

Clear and smooth like a warbler's song,
The floating melody rolls downhill.   *Shin Suk-chu*

I listen — a sad melody stirs in my heart,
I concentrate — it dispels my gloom.   *Pak P'aeng-nyon*

Always, ever, a lover looks in the mirror,
And amid vibrant silence, night deepens in the hills.
                                          Yi-Sok-hyong

Splitting a stone, limpid notes are stout,
"Plucking a Willow Branch" breaks a lover's heart.[1]
                                          Song Sam-mun

---

[1] *A "MUSIC BUREAU" SONG ACCOMPANIED BY A HORIZONTAL FLUTE; SO IS "PLUM BLOSSOMS FALL," NINE LINES LATER.*

Clear and muddy notes come in order,
the kung and shang modes unmixed.[2]   *Yi Kae*

How wonderful, notes drawn out and released,
How pleasant, reaping waves of sound.

Long since I played it seated on my bed.
Where is the zestful player leaning against the tower?
                                                       Pak P'aeng-nyon
Marvelous melodies recall Ts'ai Yen,
Who remembers Juan Chi's clear whistle?   *Yi Sok-hyong*

"Plum Blossoms Fall" in the garden,
Fishes and dragons fight in the deep sea.   *Song Sam-mun*

First, the drawn-out melody startled me,
Now I rejoice in the clear, sweet rhythm.   *Yi Kae*

How can only a reed whistle in Lung
Make the Tartar traders flee, homesick?   *Shin Suk-Chu*

On Mount Kou-shih a phoenix calls limpidly,
In the deep pool a dragon hums and dances.   *Pak P'aeng-nyon*

A wanderer is struck homesick over the pass,
A widow pines in her room.   *Yi Sok-hyong*

Floating, floating, the music turns sad,
Long, long, my thought is disquieted.   *Song Sam-mun*

We were all ears at the first notes,
But can't grasp the dying sounds.   *Yi Kae*

A startled wind rolls away the border sands,
Cold snow drives through Ch'in park.   *Shin Suk-chu*

I don't tire of your music,
Should I rise and dance to your tune?   *Pak P'aeng-nyon*

2. *THE FIRST TWO NOTES OF THE PENTATONIC SCALE.*

Who is that master flautist,
His creative talent is all his own.   *Yi Sok-hyong*

Prince Ch'iao is really not dead,
Has Huan I returned from the underworld?   *Song Sam-mun*

His solo — a whoop of a single crane,
In unison — a thousand ox-drawn carriages.   *Yi Kae*

Choking, choking, now a tearful complaint,
Murmuring, murmuring, now a tender whisper.
                                          Shin Suk-chu
I beg you, flute master,
Hide your art, don't spoil it   *Yi Sok-hyong*

Confucius heard Shao and lost his taste for meat;
I too forget to take my meal.   *Pak P'aeng-nyon*

I cannot help cherishing your art,
I set forth my deep love for you!   *Song Sam-mun*

— EXCERPTED FROM THE ANTHOLOGY OF KOREAN LITERATURE, *COMPILED AND EDITED BY* PETER H. LEE

The following three examples of linked verse portray the beautiful unfolding of the learning process through a unified effort.

OBLATION

The sharp edge of suffering has not entered my family through the door of AIDS. I slam the door and hold it tight but moans and sighs penetrate.

Am I afraid of getting what you got
or am I afraid you'll see me needing
something you have to give?

Why the fear? But
    who is free of it?
It lurks like a shadow behind
    everything: corrupts all
    possible intimacy.

Plans, Dreams never fulfilled, A Life not lived;
Death is never just, it comes leaving sadness
    in its wake.

You lay dormant so long.
If only we had realized your slumber was
        death in waiting.
Now you lie among us, your trademarks
        emaciation, weakness, pain.

    Night flowers fade
    I feel the wind mourn for you —
    don't blame yourself for being human.

My wish to soothe and help
Is in conflict with my urge to ignore the cries
and remain safely apart.

I keep hoping it will just go away
and it doesn't
and it won't until
the hatred that feeds it
dies

Can we work together to end this dark chaos,
Interconnect medical science with man's hope and unite
so that one day we may all bathe in Eternal light?

— WRITTEN BY MY ADULT CREATIVE WRITING CLASS AT METROPOLITAN LEARNING CENTER'S
COMMUNITY SCHOOLS, FALL 1988. CONTRIBUTORS (IN ORDER OF SUBMISSION): SHIRLEY
CLIFFORD, KATHLEEN B. GOLDBERG, EMERY HERMANS, MONICA SCHELB, CLARISSA M.
DEARMON, EDNA KOVACS, DOUGLAS DUNLAP, MICHAEL O'HARA, MAURICE LAFOLLETTE.

COMMUNICATION

It's really easy to talk, but at times it's difficult to put into
words how you feel. My boyfriend says words have limits,
because to say "I love you so much" means "I love you *only* so
much." So we have been teaching ourselves sign language.

Sign language — the language of the deaf. The wish, the need
to communicate when the body fails.

Touch is also sign language, releasing our intimate feelings
when words fail.

The need to read one's lips is a source of sign language for the hearing impaired.

Actions and reactions can tell all — body language another sign.

Body language so powerful, one must watch what they are saying.

More than just speaking — hand gestures add a new dimension to communication.

Open your ears to listen and your heart will follow.

Open your eyes, and perhaps your heart will see.

Close the door to communication and not only will your relationships die, but also your soul.

Without communication, nothing will ever work out, fights will never end, and "I love you" will never be said.

And we will never truly be happy if we don't have someone to love, someone to communicate with.

And what about the communication your resting mind sings to you and only you...dreams. Read the colors of your sleep, what you don't see, hear, feel may fill the cracks and empty spaces.

A dream is simply a wish made by one's heart. We don't listen to ourselves much when we're awake, so our thoughts find their way to the surface only when we are sleeping. Dreaming is our mind's way of releasing pent up fears and anxieties as well as expressing secret dreams and desires.

Dreaming is a form of communication that we have within ourselves. We need to listen and be aware. Communicating with ourselves is probably more important than communicating with others.

— WRITTEN BY THE LINFIELD COLLEGE SCHOOL OF NURSING STUDENTS IN MY COLLEGE WRITING CLASS AT GOOD SAMARITAN HOSPITAL, FALL 1992. CONTRIBUTORS (IN ORDER OF SUBMISSION): CINDY ARNOLD, PAT MATZA, DARLENE MCWRIGHTMAN, GAIL NORMAN, MICHELLE PRYOR, TRISHA WISE, HOLLY HEATON, BRANDY ELSTOEN, KELLY KILB, VANESSA BECKER, DESTINY FOGARTY, HEATHER MAE BROTHERTON, DAVINA CRAIG, CHERYL STRUCKMEIER, ANNA CORGAIN.

A to Z

IU-MIEN PROVERBS
From Southeast Asia

Read and reflect upon the following Iu-Mien proverbs that have their origins in Laos. Respond by writing a vignette, parable, prose poem, personal narrative — or any other form. Share responses. Illustrate these pearls of wisdom — or create a mural create. Add other proverbs to the list.

IU-MIEN ALPHABET PROVERB BOOK
YIU MIENH NZANGH MAC SOU

B
(FRUIT) BIOUV
Plant a tree to see the flowers. Enjoy the flowers because they will become fruit. People work hard because they fear starvation.

C
(ONION) CONG
One onion cooked with meat will change its flavor. One rotten fish will spoil a whole basket of fish. One bad person will damage the reputation of the whole group.

D
(PIG) DUNZ
To pick a piglet look at its heredity. To choose a mate look at their character.

F
(UMBRELLA) FAANX
An umbrella is to provide shade from the sun. School provides education for the ignorant.

H
(SHOES) HEH
In order to have clean feet, one must not be concerned if the shoes become worn. In order to be wealthy, one must bear hardship.

Hɪ
(Fox) Hɪᴇʜ-ᴊᴜᴠ

There are many kinds of coyotes in the forest. Some are big and some are small. Each knows its limit. Big coyotes hunt big game; small ones hunt small game.

Hʟ
(Bᴀᴍʙᴏᴏ) Hʟᴀᴜᴠ

One bamboo is not enough to make a fence. One man is not able to build his own house without help from others.

Hᴍ
(Fᴀᴄᴇ) Hᴍɪᴇɴ

Do not trust people because of their honest face and sweet talk, they may have a bitter heart.

Hɴɢ
(Sᴍᴇʟʟ) Hɴᴏᴍᴠ

In order to discover the aroma, it is necessary to smell. In order to become wealthy, it is necessary to save.

Hᴜ
(Cɪʀᴄʟᴇ) Hᴜɪɴɢ

The wider the circle one travels, the more one will experience. Three years education can compare to one season of travel.

J
(Dᴏɢ) Jᴜᴠ

A mean dog doesn't bark. An intelligent person doesn't brag.

K
(Pᴜʟʟ) Kᴇɴ

When I am little my mom pulls me. When I am older I pull my mom. Once adult, twice a child.

L
(Cᴀᴛ) Lᴏᴍʜ-ᴍɪᴜ

The cat helps the dog knock down the rice pot. But the only gratitude the cat receives is to be chased away. The field can only be plowed by the buffalo. But the gratitude he receives is a ring in his nose and a stick in his back.

M
(Hᴏʀsᴇ) Mᴀᴀᴢ

When something is found, it is not considered stealing. When a miscalculation is made, it is not considered stealing. A horse may stumble. People make mistakes.

MB
(MONKEY) MBING
Monkeys live off fruit. People live off their crops. Take what is needed. Leave what you can.

N
(BIRD) NORQUE
To know the seasons, listen to the birds sing. To know the folktales, listen to the old people.

ND
(TIGER) NDAH-MAAUH
On every mountain there is a tiger who rules the forest. In every village there is a head man who takes charge. In every nation there is a government that rules the country.

NG
(COW) NGONGH
The cow's horn may be sharp, but it cannot compare to a nail. The elephant may be big, but it will surrender itself to a little child.

NJ
(DEER) NJAIH
There is no place on earth that is empty of life. There is no place in life for the idle person.

NQ
(SHAKING) NQAMV
If one shakes a tree trunk, it will move the branches and leaves. Words are easy to say but the effect on others may be great.

NY
(CRAWL) NYORNG
A baby must crawl before it walks. One must learn everything he can from his surrounding environment in order to acquire knowledge.

NZ
(CANOE) NZANGV
The canoe can only float on the river; one can only depend on his trusted relatives.

P
(Blows) Piqv

One thousand cuts with a pocket knife is not as effective as one axe blow. Many strong people are not as effective as one wise person.

Q
(Shrimp) Qaa

A shrimp is not red unless it is cooked. One feels no shame unless a crime has been committed.

S
(Book) Sou

Planting a sapling will lead to fruit; reading books is the key to success.

T
(Ladder) Tei

Even a long ladder can never reach the sky. Even a self-sufficient person needs the help of others.

W
(Water) Wuom

Once the water is clear, the rocks will be seen. Lies will eventually become known when the truth is made clear.

Y
(Goat) Yungh

Goats can climb the cliffs, but men can climb to the moon. One may feel that he has it all, but others may have more.

Z
(Elephant) Zaangz

The elephant's body is big, but the little bird has a bigger heart. Do not judge people by their looks. Judge people by their heart.

— *David T. Lee, ESL Bilingual Program, Portland Public Schools*

A to Z

NATIVE AMERICAN
Spells, Chants, & Prayers

A FALL LULLABY

The Eternal Woman, Our Mother Earth, gives the Pueblo people their sacred food, corn. It is still planted the old way, the kernels poked into the ground with a planting stick. Corn is the staple food and every part of the plant is used. Young sprouts are boiled as greens, underdeveloped ears are made into soups, and kernels are ground into fine powder for piki bread and tortillas. The perfect ears are saved for Kiva ceremonies. All Pueblos hold corn dances to honor the spirit of the Corn Mother.

> *Now bring the Corn, Our Mother,*
> *Bring the life-giving Corn.*
> *In all our thoughts and words*
> *Let us do only good;*
> *In all our acts and words*
> *Let us be all as one.*
>
> — Pueblo Medicine Song

— Michelle Tsosie Naranjo

Write your own fall/winter/spring/summer lullaby based upon a ritual you practice that gives you the feeling of wholeness. The Navajos praised the beauty they found in all four directions. Some contemporary rituals may include canning or jamming in early fall. You may want to write a sequence of poems based upon the beautiful plants, animals, and natural phenomena you wish to praise. You may add musical accompaniment — drum, flute, percussion — and create dance steps.

In a classroom setting, write poems as you plant beans and peas. You may have a pet rabbit, goldfish, or chameleon in your classroom that would also inspire a praise poem. Chant your poems aloud.

OUR GARDEN GROWS

Outside the workshed,
we bring our shovels and seeds.
Today we're going to plant trees
and sunflowers and carrots.
Plum trees
apple trees
cherry and banana
maple trees
orange trees
walnut trees and
pear trees.
Trees will give us fruit
Trees will give us air
Trees will give us squirrels
boats and birds.
We can come here with our friends
and watch our garden grow.

— *First grade students, Mrs. Glennon-Daniel's class*

STARS

Oh stars. I love your beautiful shape.
You sparkle so beautifully. I love to
sit on my window and watch you
sparkle. I like to wish upon you. I
love to watch when you fall. I wish I
could ride on you or touch one of
you. Oh stars. You sparkle up my
night. Stars I love the way you
sparkle up the night. I wish I could
sleep on one of you. You make me
happy. I fall asleep when I look at
you. How come you fall out of the
sky?

— *Joanna Etzel, grade 2, Patti Browder's class*

A fun approach to writing a Native American song is to write an un-
rhymed couplet and repeat the verse with drums, flutes, and dance. Take for
example, the following Kwakiutl "Song of Parents Who Want To Wake Up
Their Son."

SONG OF PARENTS WHO WANT TO WAKE UP THEIR SON

Don't sleep! for your paddle fell into the water, and your spear.
Don't sleep! For the ravens and crows are flying about.

— *Reprinted from* The Sky Clears, *by A. Grove Day*

Link the writing of Native American spells, chants, and prayers to a social studies unit. Build tipis and sit shoulder-to-shoulder in a circle sharing your poems and stories aloud.

A to Z

OPENINGS AND CLOSINGS
Multicultural

Write a poem or legend using one of the Openings and Closings suggested below. Share your legends in a circle. Work individually or in small groups. Create masks, skits, songs, and dances. You may even want to make or write books to be illustrated with watercolors, charcoal, and woodblock and linoleum prints. To make your legends come to life, you can also mold or make mythical beings, plants, animals, magic drums — whatever your legend or poem suggests to you — out of clay.

The following multicultural openings and closings were collected by noted author, poet, and professional storyteller, Steve Sanfield.

OPENINGS...

Once upon a time...

Long, long ago...

There was once, in old times, and in old times it was... (Ireland)

Once upon a time and a very good time it was, tho' it was neither in my time nor in your time not in anyone else's time... (England)

Once upon a time when pigs spoke rhyme and monkeys chewed tobacco and hens took snuff to make them tough and ducks went quack quack quack-o... (England)

Time and again the tale has been told of... (Italy)

In a certain kingdom, in a certain land, in a certain village there lived... (Russia)

Once upon a time, a long, long time ago
when mice ran after cats
and lions were chased by rats... (Roumania)

In olden times when wishing still helped... (Germany)

Once there was, and once there was not, a long time ago when God had
many people but it was a sin to say so, when the camel was a town crier
and the cock was a barber, mother's cradle, tinger, minger... (Turkey)

Once upon a time, a very good time
Not my time, not your time, old people's time... (Bahamas)

To know and to tell a lie does quite well.
I walked by a creek thrashing my stick,
I went through the corner stumbling along... (Chile)

In the beginning when the world was new... (Maidu, California)

At the time when men and animals were all the same and spoke in the
same tongue... (Navajo, Arizona)

Let's throw stories... (Bandi, Liberia)

I can tell lies, too... (Tiv, Nigeria)

...CLOSINGS

...and they all lived happily ever after.

...and if they didn't live happily ever after, that's nothing to do with
you or me. (England)

...and there's no need to ask if they were happy. (Germany)

...unless they died in the meantime, they may well be there to this
very day. (Italy)

...and three apples fell from heaven; one for the storyteller, one for he
who listens, and one for he who understands. (Armenia)

That is my story. If there be a lie in it, be it so. It is not I who made it or invented it. (Ireland)

Just a tale that people will tell. (Polynesia)

No matter whether it is told or not that's the way it happened. (Japan)

May you take it and may the next one tell it better. (Ireland)

...Story. Story. (Haida, Queen Charlotte Islands)

A to Z

ORGANIC POETRY
Writing From Your Roots

What is your myth? Your country? Your Dream? Explore your own roots.
Describe yourself as a goddess or landscape. Write from within.

About the following poem, "The Dyke With No Name Thinks About
Landscape," Judith Barrington writes:

> *When teaching a writing class called "Landscape and Memory," I*
> *realized that not everyone experiences the outdoors as a nurturing*
> *place, in spite of so much writing (often by white, middle-class writ-*
> *ers) about finding spiritual comfort in the wilderness. An African-*
> *American friend was writing about what she thought were racial*
> *memories of lynchings and violence, which made it hard for her to*
> *relax in the woods, and I realized that, for me, being a lesbian had*
> *created my own alienation from nature. As a child I had felt very at*
> *home — very "natural" — in the landscape, but as an adult I had to*
> *fight bigoted ideas that labeled me "unnatural," and I read stories,*
> *like the one in section 4 of my poem, of violence that stemmed from*
> *homophobia. This led me to trace my relationship with wilderness,*
> *starting with England, where I grew up, traversing Spain and Italy,*
> *and ending up in Oregon, on the banks of the Columbia River.*

1

THE DYKE WITH NO NAME THINKS ABOUT LANDSCAPE

At first it wasn't a landscape at all.
Where you live is just where you live:

a place to walk about in,
drive your car through on the place to somewhere,

notice on a pretty day
when the clouds are puffs and grass blowing just so.

From a horse's back, tracking the skyline,
grey sea became grey sky

and chalky paths down the escarpment
gashed the smooth flank of the downs.

Leaning over to unhook the chain
of a five-bar gate, she knew

just how fast to sidle the horse through
before the metal gate swung back with a clang

and the horse twitched an ear —
too familiar with the sound to make a fuss.

The windmills, Jack and Jill, spread their sails
and grew as organic as gorse bushes

or hares on the barren plough,
but their spread sails remained unmoved

by the great wind which stirred up a great wave
in the grasses from Firle to Beachy Head.

Up there on her horse she too grew
organic as winter wheat,

never naming the villages far below:
Poynings, Ditchling, Fulking, Steyning

distant clusters of roofs that revealed to her,
as if through a telescope,

a particular lych-gate, a brick well,
a post office serving tea,

while the winding Underhill Lane,
glimpsed here and there between corpses,

whispered: *Shepherd and Dog, Wheatsheaf,
Royal Oak, The Eight Bells.*

2

When she left it became landscape —
a beloved green painting hauled around in her mind

while the next one (ochre and sage) unfolded
smelling of Mediterranean pine in the afternoon

and the one after that (sepia and umber)
threw open its chest and sang.

In these landscapes too, she wanted to grow organic —
spreading her limbs to the sky

on that almost-flat rock that jutted from the river
and held her between two swirling streams.

Pinpoints of spray pricked her skin
which dried and dried between the divided waters

while the river too — turbulence, rocks,
moss, trout, and human body —

pried open the hot thighs of the desert
with the persuasive pressure of wetness.

Was it then that it started —
then she began to feel the eyes watching?

In each landscape, people grew from the shadows.
In each landscape, people belonged.

But here on her rock,
head in the V of parted waters,

the dyke with no name sees herself
as if with eyes watching from the hill above,

sees the desert intersected by river,
sees ponderous rocks, shaggy falls, the cruising hawk,

and herself, a human figure growing from shadows,
herself in the frame, on the rock, not belonging.

3

The trouble is not nature, she thinks,
but the people who tell you there's always one of each —

starting with Noah
and his couple-filled zoo.

Pistils and stamens, winged seeds from trees,
insects waving their various appendages:

she remembers her smudgy drawings from biology;
she knows what they left out and why.

The trouble with pastoral scenes is the lovers —
the hand-in-hand, one-of-each, "lover and his lass."

She knows it's more than looking wrong in the picture.
But does she know it's a matter of life and death?

4

Whose life? Whose death?
All she wanted to do was move again like the winter wheat,

to live in her skin touching the earth's skin,
to feel spray and rock and the finger of the sun.

Once, a long time ago, she made love
on the hilltop under copper beech trees:

leaves turned to mulch underneath her
as she breathed the sky through her lover's hair

and somewhere close by a pony snickered —
a friendly snicker; an acknowledgment.

She still remembers what it felt like to lie in those arms:
some of them beech roots, others human and female,

trusting the pony like a brother,
the sky looking down the same way she looked up.

That was before the two hikers were shot —
the two women, stalked for days by the man

who killed one and left the other for dead.
One each for life and death as it turned out.

5

There is nothing organic about cars.
They skim across surfaces, separated

from the landscape by hard, black tarmac:
no danger of putting down roots.

Even when a car disintegrates in the ground,
blackberries filling the bent frame of its windshield

rusty chassis sinking into the earth
to blue up some passing hydrangea,

even then, its chrome and oil and plastic seats
spurn the comfort of ordinary rot.

The dyke with no name kept moving,
her rubber tires grabbing the blacktop with a squeal

as she pushed sideways through bends,
kept everything skidding.

Tall haystacks with poles poking out the top
dashed by her window. She noted their shape,

their resemblance to some senorita's hair
held up by a protruding pin.

She watched the show through the glass
as if she had put in her penny on the pier,

watched herself from the hillside above
speeding through picture after picture,

silk headscarf flying, arm on the door tanned,
hands turning the small leather wheel.

Sometimes, when her head raged with pain,
she parked the car in a field and slept,

all doors locked, all windows up,
while the grasses tickled the hot skin of her tires.

6

Now she is lying on a blanket, the sand below
moulded to the shape of her body.

Sudden swells slap the shore beyond her feet:
a barge has passed by,

trudging down river with its load
like a good-natured shire horse,

its throbbing lost behind the breaking
of that great wave which seems to rise from the deeps.

The turbulence is quick: a lashing of the sand
followed by September's lazy calm

as the river moves unseen again,
cows from another world low on the far shore

and the seagull's body, a fragile handful,
dangles gently between its two tremendous wings.

The trouble is not nature, she thinks
but the people who say I'm not part of it.

They're trying to paint me out of the landscape
says the dyke with no name

but her thighs in hot sand remember a horse's warm back
as the wind makes a great wave from Oregon to Beachy Head.

— JUDITH BARRINGTON

Elizabeth Woody is a Warm Springs, Wasco/Navajo Indian. Her poem, "Hand Into Stone" expresses a *re-visioning* and affirmation of the mythic power of her Native heritage after the loss of Celilo Falls on the Columbia River. This was not only a traditional gathering and fishing place, but one of the longest habitations for Indian people in North America — approximately 10,000 years until 1956, when it was sold to accommodate The Dalles Dam.

HAND INTO STONE

Some day the land will be our eyes and skin again.
— MY GRANDMOTHER, ELIZABETH PITT, 75 YEARS OLD.

Her creped fingers,
teethmarked with red speckles,
held mine tight
as she showed our finger moons to me.
They grew together as snowy stones
scratching themselves sleepily.

She had long fingers
with the mobility of spiders.
I felt them at night
as they climbed my skin.
She wrapped us
in tight shells
with agate crystals.

We breathe in our own breath
under this cover.

— *Elizabeth Woody*

Even if you're not of Native American descent, research your local library, historical society, or museum — rich with teeming facts to further explore the Native American cultural heritage.

In an introduction to her poem, "The Crown of Laurel," Ursula Le Guin writes:

> *This is what Adrienne Rich has called a re-visioning. Myths are one of our most useful techniques of living, ways of telling the world, narrating reality, but in order to be useful they must (however archetypal and collectively human their structure) be retold; and the teller makes them over — and over. Many women and some men are now engaged in what almost seems a shared undertaking of re-telling and re-thinking the myths and tales we learned as children — fables, folktales, legends, hero-stories, god-stories... Very often the re-visioning consists in a 'simple' change of point of view. It is possible that the very concept of point-of-view may be changing, may have to change, or to be changed, so that our reality can be narrated.*

THE CROWN OF LAUREL

He liked to feel my fingers in his hair.
So he pulled them off me, wove a wreath of them,
and wears it at parades and contests,
my dying fingers with their kitchen smell
interlocked around his sunny curls.
Sometimes he rests on me a while.
Aside from that, he seems to have lost interest.

It wasn't to preserve my 'virtue' that I ran!
What's a nymph like me

to do with something that belongs to men?
It's just I wasn't in the mood.
And he didn't care. It scared me.
   The little goatleg boys can't even talk,
but still they wait till they can smell you feel
like humping with a goatleg in the woods,
rolling and scratching and laughing — they can laugh! —
poor little hairycocks, I miss them.

   When we were tired of that kind of thing
my sister nymphs and I would lie around,
and talk, and tease, and stroke, and chase, and stretch
out panting for another talk, and sleep
in the warm shadows side by side
under the leaves, and all was as we pleased.

   And then the mortal hunters of the deer,
the poachers, the deciduous shepherd-boys:
they'd stop and gape and stare with owly eyes,
not even hoping, even when I smiled...
New every spring, like daffodils, those boys.
But once for forty years I met one man
up on the sheep-cropped hills of Arcady.
I kissed his wrinkles, the ravines of time
I cannot enter, grazing in his eyes, whose dark
dimmed and deepended, seeing less always, till he died.
I came to his burial. Among the villagers
I walked behind his grey-haired wife.
She could have been Time's wife, my grandmother.
   And then there were my brothers of the streams,

O my river-lovers, with their silver tongues
so sweet to thirst! the cool, prolonged delight
of a river moving in me, of his flow and flow and flow!
   They send to my roots their kindness even now,
and slowly I drink it from my mother's hands.

   So that was all I knew, until he came,
hard, bright, burning, dry, intent:
one will, instead of wantings meeting;
no center but himself, the Sun. A god
is like that, I suppose; he has to be.
But I never asked to meet a god,

let alone make love with one! Why did he think
I wanted to? And when I told him no,
what harm did he think it did to him?
It can't be hard to find a girl agape
to love a big blond blue-eyed god.
He said so, said, "You're all alike."
He's seen us all; he knows. So, why me?

I guess that maybe it was time for me
to give up going naked, and get dressed.
And it took a god to make me do it.
Mother never could. So I put on
my brown, ribbed stockings, and my underwear
of silky cambium, and my green dress.
And I became my clothing, being what I wear.

I run no more; the winds dance me.
My sister, seamstress, sovereign comes
up from the dark below the roots
to mend my clothes in April. And I stand
in my green patience in the winter rains.

He honors me, he says, to wear
my fingers turning brown and brittle, clenched
in the bright hair of his head. He sings.
My silence crowns the song.

— *Ursula K. Le Guin*

For the past three years, I have experienced great success using Le Guin's *Buffalo Gals and Other Animal Presences* as one of my college writing texts at Linfield College. My students and I have spent many thoughtful hours discussing her stories and poems, filling our own notebooks with organic lyrics and prose.

TASTE MY PLUM TOMATOES

Seed sprouting from the ground
growing, growing
into stalk and stem.
Tall, green, and serene
Small plum tomatoes bud and then flower
from my arms to my fingers.
Hard, green fruits

Warming themselves in the sun.
Soft orange juicy tomatoes
become ripe and tasty.
A woman is near.
She stretches and then prays
for all her vegetables to grow wholesome.
A woman comes near.
She plucks off one of my vegetables.
I sacrifice my fruit
for her presence.

— *Heidi Shortell, junior, education major, Linfield College, 1993*

A to Z

PASTORAL/IDYL/ECLOGUE

A pastoral is a poem about shepherds and other herdsmen or in praise of such a life as they lead, but often deceptive in its simplicity, since it may be the vehicle of a grave theme unrelated to the rural scene. An idyl, another name for the pastoral, means more specifically a short poem offering a happy picture of country life. It is associated with Theocritus, whose first idyl begins with the words of Thrysis the shepherd:

> *The whisper of the wind in*
> > *that pine-tree,*
> > > *goat-herd,*
> > *is sweet as the murmur of live water;*
> > *likewise*
> > > > *your flute-notes…*

These lines are from William Carlos Williams' version of the poem. The Greek poet's idyls furnished a model for Vergil's Eclogues and both have been widely imitated. The eclogue, also called the bucolic, is synonymous with pastoral but usually refers to a dialogue between two herdsmen. Pastoral and bucolic are also used as adjectives to describe poetry dealing sympathetically with country themes. The eclogue is apt to carry a religious or ethical message and more recently to express the poet's social philosophy.

— EXCERPTED FROM POETRY HANDBOOK: A DICTIONARY OF TERMS BY BABETTE DEUTSCH

The following eclogue, "An Arab Shepherd Is Searching for His Goat on Mount Zion" was written by Yehuda Amichai. Here Amichai lingers on the notion that peace is indeed possible — if not inevitable. Born in Wurzberg, Germany, in 1924, he grew up in an Orthodox Jewish home. His father was a shopkeeper, his grandfather a farmer, and his memories of childhood (the political situation nothwithstanding) idyllic. In 1936 he came to Palestine with his parents, and his adult life has been lived in the midst of the convulsive struggle of Israel to become a state, and then survive and define itself.

Amichai made his living as a teacher while studying war — with the British army in World War II, with the palmakh in the Israeli War of Independence in 1948, and with the Israeli army in 1956 and 1973. He was formed, as he would say, half by the ethics of his father and half by the cruelties of war.

AN ARAB SHEPHERD IS SEARCHING FOR HIS GOAT ON MOUNT ZION

An Arab shepherd is searching for his goat on Mount Zion
and on the opposite mountain I am searching
for my little boy.
An Arab shepherd and a Jewish father
both in their temporary failure.
Our voices meet above the Sultan's Pool
in the valley between us. Neither of us wants
the child or the goat to get caught in the wheels
of the terrible Had Gadya machine.

Afterward we found them among the bushes
and our voices came back inside us, laughing and crying.

Searching for a goat or a son
has always been the beginning
of a new religion in these mountains.

— YEHUDA AMICHAI

Write a modern pastoral/idyl/eclogue. If pastures and running brooks aren't within immediate reach, research the library for books, magazines, newspapers — they provide transport to places always dreamed of. Cultivate simplicity.

A to Z

PUBLIC ART
Poetry & Lyrical Prose

In the city of Portland where I live, there are wonderful opportunities to respond to works of public art via the written word.

A class field trip may be planned around public art and architecture walks. In Oregon, you may even be lucky enough to happen upon Helen Lessick's birch pergola sculpture located in the Hoyt Arboretum, or a trompe-de-l'oeil mural created by young artists from Lynn Takata's mural class at Pacific Northwest College of Art.

Wherever you live and travel, keep your eyes open for the art in public places — from the Picasso statue of "Bird Man Woman" in Chicago, to the Haida totem poles in Vancouver, British Columbia's Stanley Park. Public art is a charismatic key to understanding the indigenous culture in which it appears.

Write a poem, legend, or journal entry about the art that you see.

Metropolitan Learning Center Community School students in Edna Kovacs' Creative Writing Summer Camp explore windows into their own worlds while responding to a trompe-de-l'oeil mural, Northwest 21st and Flanders Streets, Portland, Oregon, July 1972 (photo: Edna Kovacs).

Georgia Gerber's Bear and Salmon statue, Sixth and Alder Streets, Portland, Oregon (photo: Edna Kovacs).

A to Z

QUATRAINS/RUBAIYAT
From Rumi — Illuminations
Written in Four Short Lines

Rubaiyat is the Persian word for quatrains. The following Rubaiyat by Jelaluddin Rumi are in fact improvised music. The translators, John Moyne and Coleman Barks, have tried to connect these poems with a strong line of American free-verse-spiritual poetry, such as Whitman, Roethke, Snyder, James Wright. The late Cambridge Islamicist, A.J. Arberry, himself a pioneer Rumi translator, once called for such free-verse translations.

Rumi (1207–1273) was born in Balkh, in what is now Afghanistan. He was exiled early in life by the Mongol invasions, to Konya. Following his father, he became the center of a medrese, a learning community. Konya in the mid-13th Century was, at the very least, a trilingual city. Turkish the vernacular, Persian the literary language, and Arabic the language of the Koran and religious ceremony.

Rumi lived most of his life in Konya, Turkey, which in the 13th Century was a melting-point for many cultures at the western end of the Silk Road, a connective node for Christian, Islamic, Hindu, and even Buddhist, worlds. Rumi weaves elements from these traditions into a whole, a single energy, of which these short bursts are spontaneous fragments. And like short poems from other lineages, they require a lot of emptiness, room to wander, sky, the inward space of patience and longing. Rumi's teaching in the medrese seems to have evolved in different stages: From pre-Shams discourses, to the ecstatic spontaneity of the middle of his life — the strong heart-center poetry — to the later, complex stories and lyricism and teachings, the *Mathnawi*, which occupied the last twelve years of his life.

The following four examples are from the middle period, the *Divan-i Shamsi Tabriz* (1570 pages, 42,000 lines of poetry). Rumi was thirty-seven when he met Shams in 1244, and Shams about sixty. Up until then, Rumi had been a fairly traditional mystic, one of a long line of scholars and theologians. Shams literally took Rumi's books, his intellectual brilliance, and threw them into a well to show him how he needed to live what he'd been reading.

All day and night, music,
a quiet, bright
reedsong. If it
fades, we fade.

Keep walking, though there's no place to get to.
Don't try to see through the distances.
That's not for human beings. Move within,
but don't move the way fear makes you move.

Walk to the well.
Turn as the earth and the moon turn,
circling what they love.
Whatever circles comes from the center.

I can't tell my secrets.
I have no key to that door.
Something keeps me joyful,
but I cannot say what

— *Excerpted from Rumi's Unseen Rain*

The following are three re-creations of Rumi by Indian born poet and translator, Andrew Harvey. In a collection of quatrains from *Rumi's Rubaiyat*, Harvey strives for a fusion between the directness of English and the abandon of Persian, between Rumi's quest and his own.

Run forward, the way will spring open to you.
Be destroyed, you'll be flooded with life
Humble yourself, you'll grow greater than the world
Yourself will be revealed to you, without you.

My Rock, my Flower, Flower-Rock, Rock-Flower
Dancer-Who-Does-Not-Move! Changeless Eruption!
You sever my head, and Mind grows radiant:
Push me underwater; Heart learns to talk.

From your heart to mine, secret after secret
Whose is this talk that needs no words?
A diamond tree blossoms in Nothingness
The bird of Nowhere never stops singing

— *Excerpted from Andrew Harvey's Speaking Flame*

To write a Rubaiyat, unhurried moments are needed so that the butterfly may emerge from its chrysalis. Ralph Waldo Emerson referred to these moments of exhilaration when all egotism vanishes, as "delicious awakenings."

Empty your mind. Live your joy. And allow these moments of spontaneous illumination to unfold in four short lines.

Girl reading a book. The Dalles Public Library, The Dalles, Oregon (photo: Edna Kovacs).

A to Z

RAGA
Writing With Music
Steam of Consciousness Writing
From India

The raga (or rag) is the basic form of Indian classical music. Indeed it may always have been so. There exists evidence that the raga, or a raga-like form of music, existed as early as 400 B.C. Though the instruments of ancient India differed considerably from those used today, it seems that the musical forms and structures of those times were similar to those of today, possibly differing from today's ragas no more than the ragas of modern India differ between themselves from the north to the south of the subcontinent.

Over thousands of years of musical evolution, the raga has developed into an art form capable of summoning up the most intense spiritual feelings. The listener may experience indescribably deep yearnings for something not quite defined, but which seems to be connected with the very core of the meaning of life. These feelings vary in an infinite variety of subtle ways, according to the type of raga performed, to the degree of understanding in the listener, and according of course, to the spiritual development of the performer.

Of the four main dimensions of music — harmony, melody, rhythm and timbre — harmony is, as in China, virtually nonexistent in Indian music. But, and again as in China, this lack is more than made up for in that melody, rhythm, and timbre are developed to an extraordinarily sophisticated degree. Classical Indian melody and rhythm often exceeds anything that is found in the mainstream of Western music.

Each raga has its own name which states the raga's emotional character. This might be anything from longing for a loved one, or a mixture of melancholy and hope before dawn, to a mixture of joy and affection, or meditative thoughts on one's life at the close of day.

In India, as in other cultures, specific aspects of music also hold a variety of cosmological associations. As in China there are associations between music and time cycles: each raga is linked with a particular time of day, and sometimes with a particular season. Even today, the studied Indian would consider the playing of a raga at the wrong time to be an act of gross ignorance.

For example, Puriya Kalyan is a raga associated with the early hours of the evening, is feminine in nature and expresses tenderness and love.

While the stringed (sitar, surbarhar, and vicitra vina) and wind instruments provide the melody, the drums (tabla) and other percussion instruments provide the rhythmic accompaniment.

Development of tone color or timbre occurs in phrases:
Sthayi establishes the raga;
Antara and Sanchari help to develop it and act as
links between the first and fourth, or concluding
phrase, the Abhoga.

The Rubaiyat of Rumi have been described as being raga-like in their essence by the Indian born poet, Andrew Harvey.

In listening to Indian music, the German musician Peter Hamel, advises: "For Indian music, as for the performer himself, it is much more important that the public should be able to listen with the heart...."

In other words, listening to music such as raga, it is possible to release yourself from your thoughts into a higher realm. As a poet listening to music, clarity may occur by losing yourself to the music itself.

To translate this into a writing activity, literally, the raga represents a stream of consciousness — and music acts as a communicator and multiplier of inner states.

The following Chinese legend attests to the greater, even magical possibilities of music. It tells how the music master Wen of Cheng learned to control the elements.

Master Wen was following the great Master Hsiang on his travels. For three years Master Wen touched the strings of his zither, but no melody came. Then Master Hsiang said to him: 'By all means, go home.' Putting down his instrument, Master Wen sighed, and said: 'It is not that I cannot bring a melody about. What I have in my mind does not concern strings: what I aim at is not tones. Not until I have

reached it in my heart can I express it on the instrument; therefore I
do not dare move my hand and touch the strings. But give me a short
while and then examine me.'

Some time later he returned again approached the Master Hsiang,
who inquired: 'How about your playing?'

It was spring, but when Master Wen plucked the Shang string and
accompanied it with the eighth semitone, a cool wind sprang up, and
the shrubs and trees bore fruit. Now it was autumn.

Again Master Wen plucked a string, the Chiao string and accom-
panied it with a second semitone: a languid, warm breeze appeared,
and the shrubs and trees bloomed fully.

It was now summer, but he plucked the Yu string and had the elev-
enth semitone respond, upon which hoar frost and snow came down,
the rivers and lakes freezing up.

When winter had come, he plucked the Chih string and accompa-
nied it with the fifth semitone: the sun blazed forth and the ice imme-
diately melted away.

Finally, Master Wen of Cheng sounded the Kung string and did so
in unison with the other four strings: beautiful winds murmured,
clouds of good fortune came up, there fell sweet dew, and the springs
of water welled up powerfully.

As this legend portrays, the Chinese did believe that music could influ-
ence the phenomena of nature. But they did not believe that the tones of
mortal man could be expected to literally call forth one season after another
as in this legend of Master Wen of Cheng. If we look a little more closely at
the story, bearing in mind the great tendency of the ancient Chinese mind to
gravitate towards matters spiritual, and to express itself in symbolic terms,
then a deeper meaning stands revealed to us:

The four outer strings of the zither, and the four seasons, are symbolic of
the ancient conception of the four aspects of man: his abstract mind, his
concrete mind, his emotions and his physical body. (These four were later to
be called by the alchemists of Europe, 'Fire, Air, Water and Earth.') Master
Wen could not satisfy his guru, Master Hsiang, because Wen had not yet
mastered his own four aspects of being. Hence, as one result, he cannot
perform sublime music. But he goes off, and does not return until he has
attained the full flowering of the spirituality of his heart. Now Master Wen
can play the four outer strings to great effect. Likewise, and more meaning-
fully, he has mastered, gained total control over, and can 'play' abstract and
concrete thought processes, his emotional nature, and his physical nature.

The result of this mastery of mind and body? The vital outcome is that in playing these four outer 'strings' (his four-fold nature) in unison, he has learned also to play the central Kung string (corresponding to the Higher Self or spiritual nature). From the four-sided base of the pyramid of life, he has raised himself up to the very apex of perfection. He has also attained full mastery of himself, and hence his inner genius now manifests from the heart. Hence, too, his music has attained the necessary levels of grandeur required by his guru.

The moral here is two-fold: firstly, we must master our four-fold nature before we can attain self-realization. And, secondly, only by doing so can we go on to perform music, write poetry and prose, create art — which is truly worthwhile.

— Excerpted from David Tame's The Secret Power of Music

Whether listening to the music of the sitar or Chinese zither, the bamboo flute, the sea, a waterfall — listen and respond.

A to Z

RAP POETRY
Getting the African-American Beat

THINK! WHAT IT MEANS TO LIVE…raps Lanita Duke. Rap has ushered in a world of communication that offers people a mode of expressing their editorial opinions in a language that is rhythmic and alive.

Lanita Duke writes what she calls "radical rap." Rap may be written about any issue that is relevant. It is fast becoming one of the most popular forms of group writing among youth.

WORLD OF TRASH

You wanna put trash in different colored bins
but America killed all the Indians.
This was their land when Columbus stumbled across it;
robbin' an' killin' an' stealin' was at hand.
You wanna put trash in different colored bins —
Listen, America, Custer died for your sins.

Supporting the Earth today is cool.
Questioning recycling is against the rules.
You want us to recycle to protect this investment
but all of us owe the Indians rent.
You wanna put trash in different colored bins
but America killed all the Indians.
You wanna put trash in different colored bins —
Listen, America, Custer died for your sins.

The ozone has a big hole
from years of chemical and coal.
We had to wait for all the rancor,
including a rise in skin cancer
to document this vicious hole.
Now in the future America will be the minority
and there won't be any trees.
You chopped them down to add to your crown

and placed future generations in misery.
Now we all want a stable foundation,
but we live in a very shaky nation
built on the bread of Indians —
and now you're on a recycling binge?
You wanna put trash in different colored bins
but America killed all the Indians.
You wanna put trash in different colored bins —
Listen, America, Custer died for your sins.

The spotted owl cannot howl
when you trade his life for jobs.
Human beings cannot be first.
All living things have a purpose on this Earth.
Now environmentalists don't wanna deal with race —
but they have to, or get outta my face.
You cry about the forest or the trees
But are silent about chemicals
dumped into the community.
You demand increased insulation
but many of us do not have a stake in the nation.
Our lives are violent stories to be told
many of us die before we're eighteen years old.
Young black men are killing each other at will.
Think about that before the rainforests in Brazil.
You wanna put trash in different colored bins
but America killed all the Indians.
You wanna put trash in different colored bins —
Listen, America, Custer died for your sins.

With poverty increasing by the hour,
all you can say is DOWN WITH NUCLEAR POWER?
We are not all equal.
So prepare yourself for the sequel.
We're all on the run.
The sins of the fathers are visited by the sons.
Now don't tell me about happy Indian tribes
because it's all lies!
I wish Lewis and Clark had fallen in a ditch
and Sacajawea was a snitch.
You wanna put trash in different colored bins
but America killed all the Indians.

You wanna put trash in different colored bins —
Listen, America, Custer died for your sins!
You wanna put trash in different colored bins
but America killed all the Indians.
(Growing softer to a whisper)
America killed all the Indians…
America killed all the Indians…
America killed all the Indians…

— LANITA DUKE. COPYRIGHT © 1993, LANITA DUKE, NEWS DIRECTOR/PRODUCER, GRASSROOTS NEWS, NW, P.O. BOX 12289, PORTLAND, OREGON 97212.

The following is an education rap written by a student in my Children's Literature class at Linfield College.

LISTEN UP

If you're lookin, for a reason
to stay in school,
listen up home girl —
don't be a fool.

You like all the things you see on T.V. —
the houses, the cars, and the money.

You've got to earn it to keep it
so play it straight.
Do the work, get the grades
don't count on fate.

It's your teachers who'll help you
better your mind —
teach you math, science
and even some rhyme.

So take advantage of the learnin'
they're givin' out free.
It's worth more than anything
you'll ever see on T.V.

— LIZ BEAZIZO, JUNIOR, EDUCATION MAJOR, LINFIELD COLLEGE, 1994

What's your rap? Get the beat
and go with the flow. Break
into dance and video.

A to Z

CRAFTING SONNETS

William Shakespeare penned thirty-seven plays, but many readers love him most for his sonnets.

FORM AND FUNCTION

First, it's important to know the two major types of sonnets:
*Shakespearean, rhyming abab cdcd efef gg, each quatrain progressing toward a surprising turn of events in the ending couplet.
*Petrarchan (or Italian), rhyming abbaabba in the octave and cdecde in the sestet (or cdcdcd, avoiding any couplets), with an idea presented in the octave and the turn developing slowly in the sestet.

In terms of subject matter, the Norton Anthology of Poetry *puts the English sonnets into the following categories:*
*The love poem a la Shakespeare, Barrett and just about everyone else.
*The nature poem à la Surrey, who introduced into English what we now call the Shakespearean sonnet.
*The meditative poem à la Donne, Milton and Hopkins, who introduced sprung rhythm.
*The elegiac poem à la Longfellow, the first American master sonneteer.
*The celebratory poem à la Arnold and Poe, praising people, things and often the sonnet itself (as in Wordsworth's "Scorn Not the Sonnet," which honors past members of the form).

— Excerpted from Crafting Sonnets, by Michael J. Bugeja

The following are three examples of well-crafted sonnets: Elizabeth Barrett Browning's famous Petrarchan sonnet; a contribution from Shakespeare; and a contemporary sonnet about the infamous, immoral love affair of Georg and Grete Trakl by Michael J. Bugeja, poetry editor of *Writer's Digest Magazine.*

HOW DO I LOVE THE?

How do I love thee? Let me count the ways.
I love thee to the depth and breadth and height
My soul can reach, when feeling out of sight
For the ends of Being and ideal Grace.
I love thee to the level of every day's
Most quiet need, by sun and candlelight.
I love thee freely, as men strive for Right;
I love thee purely, as they turn from Praise.
I love thee with the passion put to use
In my old griefs, and with my childhood's faith.
I love thee with a love I seemed to lose
With my lost saints, — I love thee with the breath,
Smiles, tears, of all my life! — and, if God choose,
I shall but love thee better after death.

— *Elizabeth Barrett Browning*

TO ME, FAIR FRIEND

To me, fair friend, you never can be old,
For as you were when first your eye I eyed,
Such seems your beauty still. Three winters cold
have from the forests shook three summers' pride,
Three beauteous springs to yellow autumn turned
In process of the seasons have I seen,
Three April perfumes in three hot Junes burned,
Since first I saw you fresh, which yet are green.
Ah, yet doth beauty, like a dial hand,
Steal from his figure, and no pace perceived.
So your sweet hue, which methinks still doth stand,
Hath motion, and mine eye may be deceived.
For fear of which, hear this, thou age unbred —
Ere you were born was beauty's summer dead.

— *William Shakespeare*

GRETE'S LOVERS

It was inevitable. One day you would wake
Beside him on the divan and divine the men,
The means of your escape. A venial sin,

Or venal one, the major arteries at stake;
You wanted vengeance as much as heartache.
You wanted pain: searing, psychic, genuine
Pain. So you planned the act as a tragedienne
Plans a role, casts for it. A clean break,

And you were rooming with the best friend,
The only one Georg ever had. You had him;
Then to Berlin: a bookseller, father-figure,
Patron of the arts. The better to offend
The aspiring poet, to compose his requiem
On the piano, to inspire great literature.

— MICHAEL J. BUGEJA

A to Z

THE THREE Ts
A Tapestry of
Tempo, Texture, Tone Color

Exploring the musical influences of tempo, texture, and tone color (or tim-bre) deeply enriches a poem in subtle and significant ways.

Let's look at three poems: Mary Tall Mountain's "Seahorse Music" uses tempo markings in the poem itself. Anna Kiss' "Cosmic Tapestry" invites the reader to witness a canvas where texture, tone color, and texture are stitched in with delicate clarity. And Jaan Kaplinski's "THE SAME SEA/In Us All" is painted in vibrant hues — with the bold brushstrokes of an expressionist — while the tempo of the poem rises and falls like the sea itself.

All three poems are highly visual and tactile, as well as achieving the nuances of tempo, texture, and tone color. As a reader of these poems, I hear musical interludes and visualize watercolor paintings, weavings, and photographs. Poets who paint, draw, photograph, or who are musically inclined, should explore the realm of possibilities their poems may open to them.

As a poet, you may want to listen to music or look at a work of art, and begin your poem from there. Don't be afraid of making several sketches or etudes. I have spent many many hours sketching poems from the paintings of Georgia O'Keeffe and Paul Klee — and from the music of Bartok, the shakuhachi (Japanese bamboo flute), and harp music of the Renaissance.

Mary Tall Mountain is a Koyukon Athabascan from Nulato, Alaska, now living in San Francisco. Here is her poem.

SEAHORSE MUSIC

Mail order seahorses in the belly   *con brio*
of the jet's harsh howl.
Afloat in a dark bell,
blind eyes bulging, the
male swells, surges,
thrusts forth sons.

I unpack, unwrap swaddlings,   *andante*
Breathless
pour proud wraiths
from the shipping bell
to drift safe
through amniotic water.

Desert dawn. They call, wordless.   *ritartando*
Immense my shadow
hulks over the crystal cage.
Bright stately ghosts
hook crooked tails
around pale fingers of coral.

Slim as a silver,   *allegretto*
transparent gossamer,
the solitary
surviving baby wanders
the tremulous emerald
water-garden world.

His black fearless eye   *misterioso*
encased in a pulsing shell,
dainty as a mistflower.
His song haunts the listening air,
whispers over the Sierra
to eerie dragons of ocean.

Brave, uncommon voyager,   *largo*
your sojourn brief as a dream.
Sea Mother rises answering
across her murmurous tides.
Lonely she sings you home.

— MARY TALL MOUNTAIN

GLOSSARY FOR SEAHORSE MUSIC

con brio: with spirit and vigor
andante: in a moderate tempo
ritartando: slowing gradually
allegretto: faster than andante
misterioso: shadowed, mysterious
largo: with slow solemnity

Anna Kiss was born in 1939 in a hamlet in Hungary. Kiss studied at Budap-
est University, and now teaches school in the capital. She has published nine
volumes of poetry.

COSMIC TAPESTRY

A little woman looks out the window:
the penny tree starts chinking
a little man looks out:
penny-tree penny-chinking woman
they say nothing about it to each other
because one's feeding the hawk
and the other the pigeon
and the mountains are compressed
the mountains retreat
suns set and rise
suns set and rise
the living feed the living
life gives food to life
there's always some flesh on the fishbones
seeds don't spill through the basket
they sleep in the one common bed
at the one common table
they call each other rose, gillyflower
the moon's on the cool tower of their palace
on its ardent tower the sun
silver and gold
insider their tower walls
butterfly-wing-blue
only the penny-tree changes
quivering, changing back
changing and re-changing
changing and re-changing
when the little woman looks out:
penny-tree penny-chinking woman
they say nothing about it to each other
because one of them's feeding the hawk
the other the pigeon

— *ANNA KISS*

Jaan Kaplinski was born in Tartu, Estonia, in 1941. One of Eastern Europe's most gifted poets, he is a translator, essayist, and professor. He currently resides in Tartu with his wife and son.

THE SAME
SEA
in us all
red
dark
warm

throbbing
winds from
every quarter
in the sails
of the heart

line
of foam through
white
space

questions falling
from the oar
rolling
back
on the wave
fear
behind the darkness

or the same
sea
waiting
for another

— *Jaan Kaplinski*

A to Z

USING HAND GESTURES
in Hawaiian Dance to Create
Poetry & Lyrical Prose

HULA/MELE

According to Kapualokeokalaniakea Dalire, a senior at Linfield College in McMinnville, Oregon, who is also a professional hula dancer from Kaneohe, Hawaii:

> The hula, "Hawaiian dance," goes back to the days of the old when Hawaii was ruled by Monarchs. It is a dance that expresses the words and translations to poems that when put to music make up a Hawaiian mele or song. It is a tradition that has been carried on for many generations, perpetuated and brought back to life during the reign of Hawaii's last king, Kalakaua. Nicknamed the "Merrie Monarch," Kalakaua left a deep impression upon many when he said, "The Hula is the Heartbeat of the Hawaiians. You stop the Hula; You stop the Heartbeat." Since then, the dance has gained much popularity and is being learned by many.
>
> Hula is a dance used to tell stories put to music about the gods and goddesses of Hawaii. It is a dance that involves hand motions, foot movements, and facial expression. The hula uses total body language to interpret different songs. It is also divided into two styles: Kahiko or "the ancient dance," and Auana or "modern dance." Dancers interpret the thoughts and emotions the composer writes. Many of the mele or "songs" also carry with them a Kauna, or "double meaning." Composers often use the language to talk about personal events, and when their lyrics are translated into English, they sometimes take on a different form or meaning.
>
> The following example provides a song that falls into the auana category. Liholiho, "Beautiful 'Ilima," written by the late Emma A.K. De Fries, describes the delicate petals of the 'ilima, once reserved for those of royalty and still cherished today. It is a flower lei worn with great pride and dignity.

132

LIHOLIHO	BEAUTIFUL ʻILIMA
Onaona wale ia pua	Softly fragrant is this flower
I ka mikiʼala mau ʻia	To which much attention is given
Ua hele wale a nohea	Lovely
I ka nou a ke hehau	When pelted by the cool mist
O beautiful ʻilima	
Choice of my heart	
O sweet and charming flower	
Soft and lovely to behold	

— *EMMA A.K. DE FRIES*

On this and the next page are some common hula hand gestures choreographed and photographed by Kapualokeokalaniakea Dalire.

pua/flower

ua/rain

ʻaina/land

pali/peak

kapu/sacred

kuahiwi/mountain

ke kai/ocean   mahina/moon or kala/sun

lohe/listen

ke ike/see

Kapualokeokalaniakea Dalire, whose name means "The chosen child of the widening heaven," writes:

Being of Hawaiian ancestry, the art of the hula is an important part of my life. I grew up around a family of hula dancers and song writers. My late grandmothers were major contributors to the per-petuation of the Hawaiian culture. My maternal grandmother, Mary Keolalaulani Wong, was a Kumu Hula or a teacher of the hula. My mother, Faye Pomai'aloha Dalire has followed in her footsteps along with my father, John K. "Cioci" Dalire, as well as my two sisters Kaui and Keola, and myself. We are the foundation of the Halau or Hula School. Named after my grandmother, the Halau, known as Keolalaulani Halau 'Olapa O laka is made up of some one hundred students. My paternal grandmother, the late Emma De Fries, took in my father as her own. The Hawaiians call this "Hanai" — a form of adoption without the legal paper work.

To me, Emma De Fries was "nana." To others, she was a woman of great knowledge and wisdom about the old Hawaiian ways. By naming me at birth, she enabled me to carry on the akea and De Fries name. These two very special people, one a teacher, the other a composer, have encouraged me to take pride in my culture and share it with others. All my life I have studied and danced the hula. I can honestly say that I have accomplished many of my goals in life because of it. Winning various titles and honors in hula has made me a positive role model among many younger generations of dancers. Attending college away from home has also enabled me to share my culture with others.

— KAPUALOKEOKALANIAKEA DALIRE

Use the above hand gestures from Hawaiian dance to create poems, legends, myths, stories.

A to Z

VILLANELLE
An Idyl
Written in Five Three-line Stanzas &
Ending With a Stanza of Four Lines

One of the most adaptable of the French forms, the villanelle consists of nineteen lines on two rhymes in six stanzas, the first and third lines of the opening tercet recurring alternately at the end of the other tercets, and both repeated at the close of the concluding quatrain. With the first line A and the third, which rhymes with A', the scheme is AbA', aba, abA', aba, abA', bAA'. Originally associated with pastoral verse, the villanelle has been adapted to a variety of uses by nineteenth and twentieth century poets. Take, for example, the following by Theodore Roethke.

THE WAKING

I wake to sleep, and take my waking slow.
I feel my fate in what I cannot fear.
I learn by going where I have to go.

We think by feeling. What is there to know?
I hear my being dance from ear to ear.
I wake to sleep, and take my waking slow.

Of those so close behind me, which are you?
God bless the Ground! I shall walk softly there,
And learn by going where I have to go.

Light takes the Tree; but who can tell us how?
The lowly worm climbs up a winding stair;
I wake to sleep, and take my waking slow.

Great Nature has another thing to do
To you and me; so take the lively air,
And, lovely, learn by going where to go.

This shaking keeps me steady. I should know.
What falls away is always. And is near.
I wake to sleep, and take my waking slow.
I learn by going where I have to go.

— THEODORE ROETHKE

Using a more flexible approach to an old form, Michele Glazer explores how the villanelle, with its variations and repetition of line, can make for a deeply moving poem. In fact, the departure from the true form is in itself a metaphorical statement. Michele works for The Nature Conservancy and has been widely published.

IN THE PROVINCE
    (BEN LINDER 1959–1987)

At point-blank range was not the way
Boys from our block died. Or young.
When Ben did both we were amazed.

Those first few days his name in boldface
Arrested us; the suburbs stuttered
News about the way

Ben died. Headlines praised
What, yesterday, they'd damned, flag-strung
What's left. I am amazed —

What is the nothing-of-him-that-doth-fade?
I run my open hand across his face, rub
My nose (I know some ways

Collusion grows); it leaves a black swath
That washes off.

His face foams up, now buried on page 48.
He, too, seems dazed.
My coffee's cold. He died and we remain
Amazed how small the neighborhood's become.

— MICHELE GLAZER

Of Ben Linder: From Portland, Oregon, he was a hydraulics engineer on a rural hydroelectric project in Nicaragua when he was shot to death by the Contras. Ben also was a juggler and a unicyclist. He performed in the circus in Managua, and had unicycled from Portland to Seattle and from Portland to San Francisco.

A to Z

VOICES IN POETRY & LYRICAL PROSE
Exploring Persona(s)

Twentieth century Greek poet Odysseus Elytis focuses his poems on the creation of personal mythology. In "Maria Nefeli, A Poem In Two Voices," he links a young girl's name and the region of clouds, and shapes his perceptions through the juxtaposition of her liberated "leap into ideas" and a much older persona's attempt to understand her free-wheeling vision in his more traditional terms.

In an interview with Ivar Ivask in 1975, Elytis said: "Maria Nephele means 'Maria Cloud.' Both names have a mythological connotation. But in my poem, Maria is a young modern radical of our age. My poems are usually rooted in my own experience, yet they do not transcribe actual events. "Maria Nephele" constitutes an exception. I met this girl in real life, and I suddenly wanted to write something very different...Therefore I made this girl speak in my poem and express her world-view, which is that of the young generation today. I am not against her, for I try to understand her by having us speak in parallel monologues. My conclusion in this poem is that we search basically for the same thing, but along different routes...Maria Nephele is the other half of me. Already in my poem 'The Concert of Hyacinths' I had written: 'On the other side I am the same.' So, here, I am showing the other side of myself."

This poem portrays the stunning use of persona to explore the yin/yang nexus of the creative spirit, the dialogue between self and soul, love and hate, good and evil, horizontal and vertical, passion and intellect. Exploring persona(s) is complex, demanding that the poet journey to innermost depths. It is a way of both releasing and expanding knowledge and awareness. Elytis probes art, music, religion, history, philosophies — using a variety of moods and tones — from subjective to objective, emotional and colloquial, to paint his themes.

In daily life, there are discourses that can be made about school, your job, the endless suffering among the homeless, poverty, and the war against hunger alone. Begin exploring the possibilities of working with personas by mapping out your own personal mythology. Who are you? Where have you been? Where are you going? Where would you like to be? Note the contrasts between your life and your dreams. What's keeping you from attaining them? Now begin to generate complementary people, places, emotions — and begin to engage in a parallel monologue. Explore mythology. For example, I am the morning star. On the other side, a phoenix speaks. Both sides are the same.

Remember to explore all your senses. List, cluster, and shrink for details. Be attuned to all the blizzards, moons, attics, and rainbows that are a part of your own personal journey.

Maria Nefeli says:
THE CLOUD

> *I live from day to day — who knows what tomorrow will bring.*
> *My one hand crumples up the money and the other smooths it*
>   *out*
>
> *You see weapons must speak in our chaotic times*
> *and we must align ourselves with our so-called "national ideals"*
>
> *Why are you staring at me, you scribbler — you who never wore*
>   *a soldier's uniform*
> *the art of making money is one of the martial arts also*
>
> *Go stay up all night — writing thousands of bitter verses*
> *go fill up the walls with revolutionary slogans*
>
> *The others will always see you as an intellectual*
> *and only I who love you: in my dreams I see you as a prisoner.*
>
> *Therefore, if love is truly "a common divider," as they say,*
> *I must be Maria Nefeli and you, alas, the Cloudgatherer.*

> *Inscribe yourself somewhere as well as you can and then*
>   *generously erase yourself.*

And the Other Speaker:
THE CLOUD GATHERER

> Ah how nice to be a cloudgatherer
> to write epics on your old shoes as Homer did
> not to care a bit if you please or not
> zero
>
> Unperturbed you reap unpopularity
> this way; with generosity; as if you owned
> a mint that you could close down
> firing all the personnel

in order to cultivate a poverty all your own
that no one else possesses.
At this hour when thick-skinned people in their offices
desperately glued to their phones
struggle in vain
you rise inside Love
all soiled yet agile like a chimney-sweep
then climb down from Love ready to inaugurate
a white beach of your own

without money

you undress as those who pay attention to the stars undress
and with wide strokes you swim out in order to weep freely...

It is bigamy both to love and to dream.

— ODYSSEUS ELYTIS

For primary school children, start by passing out pictures from magazines or sight word vocabulary and spontaneously matching them: wagon/
pumpkin, dog/fence. With age, language will move from the concrete to
abstract. A variation on this is to create puppets out of recycled cereal, cracker,
pasta, envelope, and shoe boxes — boxes of all shapes and sizes — and present
personas side by side. Work in teams. Students of all ages will enjoy crafting
and presenting these recycled puppet plays!

*Second grade class, South Sherman Elementary School, Grass Valley, Oregon, during an Artists-
in-Education residency I taught in April 1990 (photo: Edna Kovacs).*

A to Z

WAKA/TANKA
A Traditional Form of Japanese Poetry Written in 31 Syllables

Waka is a traditional form of Japanese poetry written in 31 syllables with the pattern 5-7-5-7-7. Master of this form was the early medieval Japanese poet Saigyo. Born in 1198 into a minor branch of the Fujiwara clan, he was exposed to the decadent court life of the capital city of Heian. At the age of twenty-three, Saigyo broke with the secular life and took Buddhist vows.

Saigyo's sadness over the collapse of society became autobiographical meditations. As he wandered to the far north, sometimes dwelling near the great monastery at Mt. Koya, other times at Mt. Yoshino, a place famous for its cherry blossoms that Saigyo called "home," he experienced loneliness, residual passions, karmic connections, responses to death, the deep nexus between man and nature — and wrote waka about what he saw. The result was what Basho found in Saigyo, "a mind both obeying and at one with nature throughout the four seasons." Out of waka, haiku was born.

yuki fureba	snow has fallen
noji mo yamaji no	Field paths and mountain
uzomorete	Burying them all
ochikochi shiranu	And I can't tell here from there:
tabi no sora kana	My journey in the midst of sky.
hitori sumu	Here I huddle, alone,
katayama kage no	In the mountain's shadow, needing
tomo nare ya	Some companion somehow:
arashi ni haruru	The cold, biting rains pass off
fuyu no yo no tsuki	And give me the winter moon.

asaku ideshi	The mind for truth
kokoro no mizu ya	Begins like a stream, shallow
tatauran	At first, but then
sumiyuku mama ni	Adds more and more depth
fukaku naru kana	While gaining greater clarity.

— *SAIGYO*

Read and reflect upon the above Waka/Tanka. Close your eyes. Think about the moon, the sun, the infinite stars that glow in our cosmos. Breathe in and out. Now open your eyes. Find a good writing spot. Let your meditations flow like a river. Then refine your meditations into waka form. It will be simple if you write from your heart.

A to Z

WELSH ENGLYN
Exploring Cross-rhyme

Englyn is the name given to certain tercets or quatrains, each having a distinctive syllabic form and rhyme scheme. The simplest is the "soldiers' englyn," a rhymed tercet in which each line has seven syllables. Among other devices, Welsh verse is apt to include light rhyme and cross-rhyme. This is not to be confused with crossed rhyme, and indeed is a more delicate echo. Cross-rhyme occurs when the syllable at the end of one line rhymes with a syllable in the middle of the line following. In Green Armor on Green Ground, *Rolphe Humphries presents English poems composed in the twenty-four official Welsh metres and indicates the requirements of each. His englyn, "For a Wordfarer," is patterned on quatrains made of two seven-syllable lines, a ten-syllable line and a six-syllable line, the first, second, and fourth lines rhyming, the third line cross-rhyming with the fourth. The pattern is illustrated in the stanza that follows.*

Sing them low, or say them soft.
Such a little while is left
To counterpoint the soundless drift of Time,
Let rhyming fall and lift.

— ROLPHE HUMPHRIES, EXCERPTED FROM POETRY HANDBOOK: A DICTIONARY OF TERMS BY BABETTE DEUTSCH

A to Z

FROM XANADU TO TIMBUKTU
Poetry & Lyrical Prose
Inspired by Place-names & Spirit
of Place

Whenever I travel, I seem to fall in love with places. Sometimes the name of a town on a map will draw me to it, and I'll travel out of my way just to see Mist, Azalea, Lebanon, or Lostine — all in Oregon.

Often when I ask students to write about their dream places — that locale or locales where they feel connected — a sequence of place-name poems may evolve. For example, one fourth grade student at Colonel Wright Elementary School told me his special spot was at The Underground Pizza Parlor in The Dalles, Oregon. Another student found herself happiest at the Coliseum watching a Trail Blazers' game. Haystack Rock on the Oregon coast and Disneyland were other favorite places.

PHOTOWRITING

If you have a camera and enjoy taking photographs, writing poems about places you and your family have visited — or taking a special trip, say, to the Japanese Gardens to photograph the irises in bloom — is a delightful project. Parents and children I worked with at a local community center discovered they could all write poems and vignettes from the memories prompted by the photographs. Feel free to explore free and structured forms of poetry such as acrostics, ballads, cinquains, or haiku.

Place-name poems may be linked to history, geography, and science lessons such as the Oregon Trail, the planets, and volcanos.

Following is a place-name poem written by Estonian poet Jaan Kaplinski. In an introduction to this anthropological-ecological poet's *The Same Sea In Us All*, the poet and essayist Sam Hamill writes:

> *Estonia is a tiny country bordering the east coast of the Gulf of Finland. It is the westernmost representative of non-western mental-*

ity, its language being Finno-Ugric, most closely related to Finnish. Its citizens have endured over eight hundred years of imposed government. Following the fall of Czarist Russia in 1917, Estonia established its independence and was admitted to the League of Nations in 1921. But Estonian national integrity fell victim to the Russo-German Non-Aggression Pact of 1940, and Russia established military bases there immediately. Germany occupied the country from 1941 to 1944, but with the collapse of The Third Reich, Estonia was returned to the hands of Stalinist Russia.

Jaan Kaplinski was born in Tartu, Estonia, in 1941, son of a Polish father and an Estonian mother. His father disappeared into Stalin's labor camps while Kaplinski was still a small child. He studied Romance Languages and structural and mathematical linguistics at Tartu State University, and has since been a student of anthropology and is a serious student of Mahayana Buddhism as well.

Since Kaplinski comes from a country in which 75 percent of the land is under cultivation, it is hardly surprising to hear him remark, "To occupy oneself with biology and nature in practice as well as in theory is a vast and noble undertaking. This begins with the observation of nature: photographing birds, feeding animals, describing plants; and ends with a universal science of nature which transforms the world into what I have previously called Utopia, and what was formerly called the realm of peace, The Golden Age." ...If, in his poems, Kaplinski calls for the "naturalization of people," it is because he knows, as our own Robinson Jeffers did, that we cannot long stand apart.

BALLAD OF MARY'S OWN LAND*

No strength any more: Sakala weakens, Nurmekund sways,
sated ravens above us, and beneath us sooty snows.

The fortress of Ravala rises high over the flashing flood.
The city is alien and large, and alien, too, is your blood

and Oandi and Oteppaa. There you stop on the billowing road.
Hammering sounds from the hilltops, orders in foreign words.

Look over the sea and the forests, watch places and names disappear.
Look at Vaiga as long as you can while Alutagase is still here.

One random shriek of an eagle, the flight of the one-day moth —
if you lose your songs and your language, it is total loss.

Wait a while. The lakes will vanish; from the sea, the coast will rise,
salt sea water will eat out your heart and rust away your eyes;

sunk to the salty bottom, you sleep under crumbling ice.
The engines of siege are dragged to Saarde over your sunken face.

— JAAN KAPLINSKI (*ALL NAMES ARE OF PLACES)

Spirit of place is captivated here in quatrain form by Hiroko Yamada in her poem about a visit to Ladakh, near Nepal.

LADAKH

I peep into the picture.
They are living.
For what?
They are living to live.

Wearing hats carved strangely.
Selling the vegetables.
Smiling happily.
Walking thoughtfully.

The village turned into white.
A man was walking with a bull in the snow.
Their faces are like an apple.
Do you feel cold?

They pray.
What are you praying?
They play.
What are the sounds like?

I saw the festival.
So many people.
So many Gods.
So many evils.

They get sunburned.
But it still seems cold.
Sadness? — No!
Miserable? — No!

There is not much green.
They are like sand castles

under the blue sky
beside the white mountain.

Winter has come again.
So calm.
Crows are crying.
Still they are living to live.

— Hɪʀᴏᴋᴏ Yᴀᴍᴀᴅᴀ, Tᴏᴄʜɪɢʜɪ, Jᴀᴘᴀɴ, ɪɴᴛᴇʀɴᴀᴛɪᴏɴᴀʟ sᴛᴜᴅᴇɴᴛ, Lɪɴꜰɪᴇʟᴅ Cᴏʟʟᴇɢᴇ, 1992

Here's a place-name poem I wrote about a beaver I met one morning on the outskirts of the Quinault Indian Reservation in Moclips, Washington.

THE BEAVER

Walking through Moclips,
I meet a man pointing at something.
On his lips, I can
just make out the words:

    "There's a beaver over here."

I cross the road.
In the creek
a beaver swims
branch fixed
between its teeth
threads of brown fur
matted back
so you can see its
coal brown eyes.

The old man tips his cap,
whispers through the silklike mist,

    "I see him on my walks."

    "Sure wouldn't wanna swim in that,"
I whisper back.

    "Naw, it's cedar water —
black as oil."

The beaver swims towards us
full-faced. I peer into
the murky inlet
full of yearning.
It's the first beaver

I've ever seen.
Not even seven,
the SURF EDGE GROCERY
isn't open yet,
and the girl who sells
blackberries
for a penny apiece
is still asleep.

— *Edna Kovacs, July 1988*

"Life is a perpetual journey," wrote Walt Whitman. Wherever you travel, always take your notebook with you, your camera, and your imagination hat. Write from within.

A to Z
YARNING
A 99-word Short Story

Tell a story in 99 words or less. It may be fact or fiction. Create a pseudonym for yourself which fits the composition. Include a Who? What? When? Where? and Why? Remember to count all articles. And don't forget to include a title.

WHAT LATRELLE TOLD ME

Over coffee, in the BRANDING IRON CAFE, he begins:
"In Bitterfield, West Germany, nothing grows anymore. It's a nuclear waste field, a chemical paradise, but the children still drink the milk that comes from cows that graze on the land."
I look out the window. Here, in Grass Valley, April wheat glows verdant. The wind turns cartwheels. Tumbleweed skips.
"Until the air is still, the flappers won't be spraying," he whispers, so as not to be overheard.
The waitress refills our coffee cups, whistling, "How Can I Be Sure, In A World That's Constantly Changing?"

— EDNA KOVACS/ALIAS "SALLY DESCHUTES," APRIL 1990, FIRST PLACE WINNER OF WRITER'S NW'S BREVELOQUENCE (99-WORD SHORT STORY) CONTEST

In March 1991, I worked with a group of primary school children at Arbor School, Tualatin, Oregon, on the creation of Native American legends. The following is a 99-word legend created by Naomi Cole.

THE STAR DANCE

Once there was a little girl. She loved the stars and she loved to dance to the stars. Her name was Little Star and she had a doll named Bright Star. Little Star had a tipi. She set up her doll in it. She painted it with stars. One night she danced in the starlight. She danced around the fire. She looked up at the stars. She had loved the stars ever since she was a baby. She loved the bright stars at night, and that is how she got her name: Little Star.

— NAOMI COLE/ALIAS "LITTLE DOLL," GRADE 3

A to Z
YOUR HOLIDAYS
In Poetry & Lyrical Prose

Like calendar poetry, another enjoyable writing project is the creation of holiday poems, centered around a particular occasion. In school, or at home, with family and friends, try making your own Halloween, Christmas, or Valentine's Day cards.

The following two examples portray the inspiration that comes from the Japanese and Celtic people's traditional observance of All Souls Night and of the Jewish people's celebration of Spring through T'u B'Shavat, which is The New Year of the Trees.

Loreena McKennitt says of her song that follows that it "was inspired by the imagery of a Japanese tradition which celebrates the souls of the departed by sending candle-lit lanterns out on waterways leading to the ocean, sometimes in little boats; along with the imagery of the Celtic All Souls Night celebrations, at which huge bonfires were lit not only to mark the new year, but to warm the souls of the departed."

ALL SOULS NIGHTS

> Bonfires dot the rolling hillsides
> figures dance around and around
> to drums that pulse out echoes of darkness
> moving to the pagan sound.
>
> Somewhere in a hidden memory
> images float before my eyes
> of fragrant nights of straw and bonfires
> and dancing till the next sunrise.
>
> CHORUS:
> I can see the lights in the distance
> trembling in the dark cloak of night
> Candles and lanterns are dancing, dancing
> a waltz on All Souls Night.

Figures of cornstalks bend in the shadows
help up tall as flames leap high
The green knight holds the holy bush
to mark where the old year passes by.

CHORUS

Bonfires dot the rolling hillsides
figures dance around and around
to drums that pulse out echoes of darkness
and moving to the pagan sound.

Standing on the bridge that crosses
the river that goes out to the sea
the wind is full of a thousand voices
they pass by the bridge and me.

CHORUS

— Loreena McKennitt

T'u B'Shavat, The New Year of the Trees, is celebrated by Jews throughout the world. This festive holiday is marked by eating fruits that grow in Israel, such as figs, dates, and pomegranates. In Israel, it is regarded above all as a children's holiday, and it is the custom for children to plant saplings.

THE NEW YEAR OF THE TREES

It is the New Year of the Trees, but here
the ground is frozen under the crust of snow.
The trees snooze, their buds tight as nuts.
Rhododendron leaves roll up their stiff scrolls.

In the white and green north of the diaspora
I am stirred by a season that will not arrive
for six weeks, as wines on far continents prickle
to bubbles when their native vines bloom.

What blossoms here are birds jostling
at feeders, pecking sunflower seeds
and millet through the snow: tulip red
cardinal, daffodil finch, larkspur jay,

the pansybed of sparrows and juncos, all hungry.
They too are planters of trees, spreading seeds

of favorites along fences. On the earth closed
to us as a book in a language we cannot

yet read, the seeds, the bulbs, the eggs
of the fervid green year await release.
Over them on February's cold table I spread
a feast. Wings rustle like summer leaves.

— *Marge Piercy*

A to Z

ZEN POETRY
Being in the Moment

These poems and meditations, often written in gusts of between five and fifteen per sitting, are meant to be written out in your own hand on slips of paper and then hung willy-nilly on door jamb or window sill — may be tied loosely to the limb of a tree — wherever the wind can reach them. They should stay there until they disappear, or are stolen, or mysteriously go someplace else. And, some days after reading them, you may find your arms rising lightly from your sides.

Here we experience two Zen poems by Peter Levitt, a longtime teacher, poet, translator, and meditator in the Zen tradition.

WALKING WITHOUT ARRIVING

Every morning I walk up
the long road into the mountain,
every evening I walk back down.
One day a friend comes to see me.
"If you keep this up," he says,
"you'll never get anywhere."
You know, I think he's right!

— PETER LEVITT

Today I return to the river,
her waters
breathe to me —
You are home.

— PETER LEVITT

These clear reflections may be accompanied by brush-stroke paintings, watercolors, photographs, or music.

A to Z

ZOO POETRY
Lions & Tigers & Bears, Oh My!

In the fair city of Portland, our zoo holds an annual Valentine poetry contest. Students of all ages are invited to submit in several categories: ESL; preschool and kindergarten; special education; and grades 1 through 12 (divided into two year increments for judging purposes). Judges also choose an Ecology Award, a Judges' Award (if there's merit), and the Penny Avila Award.

The Washington Park Zoo Valentine Contest was originally conceived in 1976 by the late Penny Avila, a much loved local poet. The first contest had 1,592 entries. The entries have grown each year, and 17 years later, the contest had nearly 5,000 entries. Entries come from throughout Oregon and southwest Washington.

Each year the winning poems are published in an anthology from which the winners read their works around Valentine's Day at the zoo. Since 1992, they have also read their poems at LitEruption, Portland's annual book fair.

It took 20 judges from various writing organizations and colleges to choose this year's winners. The following are four poems selected from the winners of the 1993 Washington Park Zoo Valentine Contest.

So get out your safari hat and take a trip to your local zoo! Whether it's a school field trip or a family outing, you will have a lot of fun looking at the animals and writing zoo poetry!

SIGHTS OF THE ZOO

What a joyous sight; the zoo.
The collection of animals from throughout the world.
Come see the crawlers, hoppers, and lazy walkers.
Come see the flappers, fliers, and glorious soarers.
Come see the swimmers, divers, and graceful gliders.
Come see the choppers, waddlers, and skillful swingers.
Come see the roarers peepers, and silly squawkers.
Come see the strange, the beautiful, and the furry.
Come see the proud, the lonely, and the fierce.

But most of all come see me,
And we shall watch the animals' world together.
Let us see and learn together, how the creatures in this
oasis of a world, live!

— MICAH T. RUSSELL, GRADE 8, J.W. POYNTER JUNIOR HIGH SCHOOL, HILLSBORO, OREGON,
PENNY AVILA AWARD

BIG, BIG ELEPHANTS

Elephants go boom, boom with their plain flat feet
I feel big when I see one.
Slowly, slowly, slowly they pick up light straw
With their long J-shaped trunk.
Their ears look like pigs', but bigger, moving like
flags.

— VANESSA TAYLOR, GRADE K, PETER BOSCOW ELEMENTARY SCHOOL, HILLSBORO, OREGON,
FIRST PLACE WINNER PRE-SCHOOL/KINDERGARTEN

— ESTELLE KONRAD, GRADE 2, THE LEARNING WORKSHOP, FOREST GROVE, OREGON

GIRAFFE

Ancient explorers found you on the plains of Africa.
"What a puzzling animal!
Long legs, head in the sky nibbling the treetops.
Spots like a leopard, face like a camel.
Galloping across the plains.
What shall we call this graceful animal?
Ladder neck?
Stilt legs?
Camel leopard?"

— LIDIA BELCIUG, GRADE 4, ALDER ELEMENTARY SCHOOL, PORTLAND, OREGON, FIRST PLACE
WINNER ESL

— *Julie Williams, grade 5, Laurelhurst Elementary, Portland, Oregon*

SKUNKS

Skunks are cute
but they
do stink.
They have fur as
black as ink.
If in danger from a
foe, he'll lift his
tail and then he'll
go.
He stays and
sprays to make
his point.
Everyone will
flee the joint.

— *Angela Bordeaux, grade 10, David Douglas High School, Portland, Oregon, First Place, Judges' Award*

RIGHTS AND PERMISSIONS

Shin Suk-chu, Pak P'aeng-nyon, and Yi Sok-hyong reprinted from the *Anthology of Korean Literature, from Early Times to the Nineteenth Century.* Compiled and Edited by Peter H. Lee. Copyright © 1981. Reprinted with permission of the University of Hawaii Press, Honolulu.

IU-MIEN PROVERBS FROM SOUTHEAST ASIA
David T. Lee: For *Mien Alphabet Proverb Book.* Copyright © 1989 by David T. Lee. *Mien Alphabet Proverb Book* was first published through a Transitional Grant, Title VII, US Department of Education to the Portland Public Schools' ESL Bilingual Project, Project G.O.A.L., Sally Anderson, Project Coordinator and Barbara Trotter, Resource Teacher. Written by David T. Lee and Illustrated by Tien Nguyen. Reprinted by permission of David T. Lee.

NATIVE AMERICAN SPELL, CHANTS, & PRAYERS
Wintercount: For "A Fall Lullaby" by Michelle Tsosie Naranjoand "The Pueblo Medicine Song" reprinted with permission of Wintercount, American Indian Art, Prose, and Poetry, New Castle, Colorado.
University of Nebraska Press: For "Song of Parents Who Want to Wake up Their Son" reprinted from *The Sky Clears,* edited by A. Grove Day, by permission of the University of Nebraska Press. Copyright © 1951 by A. Grove Day.

OPENINGS AND CLOSINGS, MULTICULTURAL
Steve Sanfield: For "Openings and Closings." Copyright © 1993 by Steve Sanfield. Reprinted by permission of the author.

ORGANIC POETRY, WRITING FROM YOUR ROOTS
Judith Barrington: For "The Dyke With No Name Thinks About Landscape." Copyright © 1993 by Judith Barrington reprinted by permission of the author.
Elizabeth Woody: For "Hand Into Stone." Copyright © 1989, by Elizabeth Woody. Reprinted from *Hand Into Stone: Poems* by Elizabeth Woody. Reprinted with permission of the author.
Ursula K. Le Guin: For "The Crown of Laurel." First appeared in *Buffalo Gals and Other Animal Presences* by Ursula K. Le Guin, Capra Press/New American Library, 1987. Copyright © 1987 by Ursula K. Le Guin. Reprinted by permission of the author.

PASTORAL/IDYL/ECLOGUE
HarperCollins Publishers: For excerpts from *Poetry Handbook: A Dictionary of Terms* by Babette Deutsch. Copyright ©1974, 1969, 1962, 1957 by Babette Deutsch. Reprinted by permission of HarperCollins Publishers, Inc. Reprinted by permission of HarperCollins Publishers, Inc.

VILLANELLE, AN IDYL...
    Doubleday: For "Waking." Copyright © 1948 by Theodore Roethke, from The Collected Poems of Theodore Roethke. Used by permission of Doubleday, a division of Bantam Doubleday Dell Publishing Group, Inc.
    Michele Glazer: For "In the Province." Copyright © 1993 by Michele Glazer. Reprinted by permission of the author.

VOICES IN POETRY & LYRICAL PROSE, EXPLORING PERSONA(S)
    Penguin USA: For "The Cloud" and "The Cloudgatherer" from *Odysseus Elytis: Selected Poems* by Odysseus Elytis, translated by Edmund Keeley and Philip Sherrard, et al. Translation copyright © 1981 by Edmund Keeley and Philip Sherrard. Used by permission of Viking Penguin, a division of Penguin Books USA Inc.

WAKA/TANKA, A TRADITIONAL FORM OF JAPANESE POETRY...
    New Directions Publishing Corporation: For *Saigyo: Mirror For The Moon.* Copyright © 1978 by William La Fleur. Reprinted by permission of New Directions Publishing Corporation.

WELSH ENGLYN, EXPLORING CROSS-RHYME
    HarperCollins Publishers: For excerpts from *Poetry Handbook: A Dictionary of Terms* by Babette Deutsch. Copyright ©1974, 1969, 1962, 1957 by Babette Deutsch. Reprinted by permission of HarperCollins Publishers, Inc.

FROM XANADU TO TIMBUKTU...
    HarperCollins Publishers: For "An Arab shepherd is Searching for His Goat on Mount Zion from *Selected Poetry of Yehuda Amichai* by Chana Bloch & Stephen Mitchell. Copyright © 1986 by Chana Bloch and Stephen Mitchell. Reprinted by permission of HarperCollins Publishers, Inc.
    Edna Kovacs: For "The Beaver." Copyright © 1993. Reprinted by permission of the author.

YARNING, A 99-WORD SHORT STORY
    Edna Kovacs: For "What Latrelle Told Me." Copyright © 1993. Reprinted by permission of the author.

YOUR HOLIDAYS IN POETRY & LYRICAL PROSE
    Quinlan Road: For "All Soul's Night" by Loreena McKennitt. Copyright © 1993. Reprinted with permission of Loreena McKennitt and Quinlan Road Limited.
    Alfred A. Knopf, Inc.: For "The New Year of the Trees," from *Available Light* by Marge Piercy." Copyright © 1988 by Middlemarsh, Inc. Reprinted by permission of Alfred A. Knopf, Inc.

CONTRIBUTORS

Joyous thanks go out to all the students, writers, poets, and others whose work is included in this book. The list that follows is in their order of appearance in the book. Where an individual has been included more than once within the space of a chapter, there is only one listing. My apologies to those whose last names went unrecorded and to all the wonderful teachers whose students are included but whose own names are not in this list. Likewise my regrets for any other inadvertent omissions here of those recognized in the text.